real-life décor

real-life decor

100 Easy DIY Projects

to Brighten Your Home

on a Budget

by Jean Nayar

POINTclick**HOME**

Copyright © 2010 Filipacchi Publishing,
a division of Hachette Filipacchi Media U.S., Inc.

First published in 2010 in the United States
of America by Filipacchi Publishing
1633 Broadway
New York, NY 10019

PointClickHome.com is a registered trademark of Hachette Filipacchi Media U.S., Inc.

Design: Beatrice Schafroth
Editor: Lauren Kuczala
Production: Lynn Scaglione and Annie Andres

ISBN-13: 978-1-933231-70-9
Library of Congress Control Number: 2009938281

Printed in China

contents

furniture fix-ups

Just because an old table or chair is worn around

the edges and showing its age doesn't mean it has to

be shown the door. Sometimes all it takes to breathe

new life into a tired piece of furniture is a simple update.

Unless a leg is broken or a spring has sprung, a thrift-shop

nightstand or tag-sale sofa can often be transformed from

a forgotten castoff into a vibrant centerpiece with little

more than a fresh coat of paint or a new slipcover.

scandinavian-style seat

skill level: beginner

MATERIALS

- old wooden chair with padded seat
- screwdriver
- sandpaper
- tack cloth
- paintbrush
- wood primer
- white acrylic spray paint
- yardstick
- heavy cotton batting
- scissors
- upholstery fabric
- 1-inch-thick foam, cut to size of chair seat
- heavy-duty stapler
- 4 small L brackets (optional)

Transform a humdrum side chair into a charming Scandinavian-style seat with a coat of paint and new seat cover. The padded seats on most chairs, including this one, simply pop out. Just use a staple gun to attach the new fabric to the bottom of the seat and slide it back into place.

DIRECTIONS

1. Remove padded seat from chair by unscrewing it from underneath. Remove old fabric and batting, but reserve wood seat.

2. Sand all wood surfaces to remove old finish; remove dust with tack cloth.

3. Coat chair with primer; let dry. Apply several coats of white paint to chair, keeping spray can moving as you work to prevent drips and letting paint dry after each coat.

4. Measure seat pad length and width. Add 7 inches to each measurement. Cut two layers of batting to these measurements. Also cut a piece of fabric 2 inches larger than batting all around.

5. Place one layer of batting facedown on work surface; center foam, then wood seat, facedown on batting. Staple opposite sides of batting to wood, pulling it taut and even. Staple remaining sides of batting to wood in same manner. At each corner, fold in batting fullness, then staple in place. Staple additional batting layer in place in the same manner.

6. Place fabric facedown on work surface; center padded seat foam-side down on batting. Staple fabric to wood in same manner, forming neat folds or inverted pleats at corners. Trim away excess fabric.

7. Screw seat back in place on chair, using L brackets if needed.

stenciled barstool

skill level: beginner

*A playful hummingbird gives an old chair
a personal touch. Center a ready-made stencil
on a white-painted chair back and dab yellow
paint in the cutout. Or personalize it by
borrowing a motif from curtains or cushions
and purchasing a stencil to match.*

MATERIALS

- wooden chair
- sandpaper
- tack cloth
- paintbrushes
- Plaid FolkArt acrylic paints
  in White, Gold
- hummingbird stencil,
  about 3 inches high
- stencil adhesive
- stencil brush
- polyurethane sealer

DIRECTIONS

1. Remove any finish from chair; sand all surfaces. Wipe off dust with tack cloth.

2. Apply two or more coats of white paint to entire chair, letting dry after each coat.

3. Spray back of stencil with adhesive; position on backrest and smooth from center out.

4. Pounce stencil brush in gold paint, then over stencil, working from edges to center. Remove stencil; let dry.

5. Apply two or more coats of sealer to entire chair, letting dry after each coat.

upholstered footstool

skill level: beginner

MATERIALS

- old wooden stool with padded top
- screwdriver
- sandpaper
- tack cloth
- paintbrush
- wood primer
- white acrylic spray paint
- yardstick
- heavy cotton batting
- scissors
- upholstery fabric
- 2-inch-thick foam, cut to size of stool top
- heavy-duty stapler
- 4 small L brackets (optional)

Create a charming footstool with nothing more than a can of paint and a yard of fabric. To revive this tired bench, we coated the dark brown wooden base with crisp white paint and re-covered its tattered seat with a playful print.

DIRECTIONS

1. Remove padded top from stool by unscrewing it from underneath. Remove old fabric and batting, but reserve wood top.

2. Sand all wood surfaces to remove old finish; remove dust with tack cloth.

3. Coat stool with primer; let dry. Apply several coats of white paint to stool, keeping spray can moving as you work to prevent drips and letting paint dry after each coat.

4. Measure seat pad length and width. Add 9 inches to each measurement. Cut two layers of batting to these measurements. Also cut a piece of fabric 2 inches larger than batting all around.

5. Place one layer of batting facedown on work surface; center foam, then wood top, facedown on batting. Staple opposite sides of batting to wood, pulling it taut and even. Staple remaining sides of batting to wood in same manner. At each corner, fold in batting fullness, then staple in place. Staple additional batting layer in place in same manner.

6. Place fabric facedown on work surface; center padded top foam-side down on batting. Staple fabric to wood in same manner, forming neat folded inverted pleats at corners. Trim away excess fabric.

7. Screw top back in place on stool, using L brackets if needed.

upholstered side chair

skill level: beginner

MATERIALS

- wooden chair with cushioned seat
- screwdriver
- fine-grit sandpaper
- tack cloth
- paintbrush
- wood primer
- acrylic paint in desired color
- thick quilt batting (we used rolled polyester batting from Fairfield Processing)
- air-soluble fabric marker
- scissors
- tape measure
- heavyweight upholstery fabric
- T-pins
- staple gun
- clear plastic ruler
- hand drill with very narrow bit
- ½-inch-wide trim
- clear glue
- decorative upholstery nails
- plastic-tipped hammer (we used Osborne No. 36 Fancy Nail Hammer)

Give an old chair new life with a simple do-it-yourself reupholstering. After covering the seat with a fresh new fabric, accent the bottom edge with two layers of woven trim embellished with ornamental daisy tacks that echo the fabric's floral motif.

DIRECTIONS **NOTE: If wood portion of chair is in good condition, skip sanding and painting in Step 1, below.**

1. Remove cushion from chair. Lightly sand chair; wipe off dust with tack cloth. Apply two coats of primer to chair; let dry and lightly sand after each coat. Apply two coats of paint to chair; let dry and lightly sand after first coat.

2. Place cushion facedown on double layer of batting; trace around cushion. Cut out both layers of batting at the same time, adding 3 inches all around.

3. Place cushion on chair, but do not reattach. Center batting on cushion. Mark corners where cushion meets chair back; cut away squares of batting at back corners so batting lies flat on cushion.

4. Place fabric over cushion, centering pattern. Using T-pins, attach fabric in several spots.

5. Remove fabric and cushion; place facedown. Trace cushion outline onto fabric; remove pins. Cut out fabric, adding 3 inches all around.

6. Reattach cushion to chair. Center batting on cushion. Pull batting taut from side to side and staple to chair frame, just below cushion. Pull taut from front to back and staple to frame. Continue pulling and stapling batting to chair about 2 inches apart, stopping about 3 inches from front corners.

7. At front corners, smooth batting flat; staple to chair. Trim batting just past staples all around.

8. Center fabric, right side up, over batting. Pull and staple fabric to chair in same manner, placing staples just below batting staples.

9. At front corners, refer to photo (left), to form pleats in fabric. Staple to chair. At back corners, slash fabric diagonally about 3 inches. Fold under fabric at slashed corners to fit around back and staple to chair. Trim fabric just past staples.

10. Set chair on its back, with front edge of seat facing upward. Mark decorative nail placement, placing one mark at center front, one about 1 inch from each corner and spacing two or three additional marks evenly between these marks. Use ruler to keep marks aligned.

11. Place chair on one side, then the other and then on its front, to mark nail placement on sides and back same as for front. Using bit slightly smaller than nail's point, drill pilot holes about 1/4 inch deep at marks.

12. At base of chair seat, measure from one back chair leg around front of chair to other back chair leg. Add 2 inches and cut trim to this measurement, dabbing glue to ends to prevent raveling. Starting at center front of chair, place center of trim over fabric staples. Lift trim to push nails through trim into holes, working from center to back corners on each side. Use hammer to lightly tap nails flush with chair surface. If nails are not tight in holes, remove and dab glue on point before reinserting. At back legs, turn under trim ends 1 inch; nail ends in place.

13. Starting at center back of chair, place and nail trim along back edge in same manner, turning under trim ends and nailing in place near legs.

handy stepstool

skill level: intermediate

MATERIALS

- one 8-foot-long 1x12 pine board
- yardstick
- pencil
- adjustable table saw (preferably with router attachments)
- C-clamps
- compass
- drill with $\frac{1}{16}$-inch and $\frac{1}{2}$-inch bits
- jigsaw
- palm sander and drum sander or medium- and fine-grit sandpaper
- tack cloth
- #6, 2½-inch-long flathead screws
- putty knife
- wood filler
- 2-inch paintbrushes
- primer
- paint
- satin polyurethane

SIZE: 24X12X12 INCHES

A bold color and a simple design make this handy stepstool as stylish as it is practical. In fact, it's so good-looking you won't want to put it away between uses.

NOTE: For all of our wood projects we used the Skil Xshop convertible work bench, 4390 jigsaw and/or 7490 palm sander, all from Skil Tools.

DIRECTIONS

1. Measure and mark three 24-inch-long pieces of 1x12 board. Using the table saw, cut the pieces as marked. If you're using a circular saw, jigsaw or hand saw, clamp the board to your work surface before cutting.

2. Choose the piece with the fewest knots and nicks for the top of your stool. Measure and mark the center of the board. Measure and mark two 3½-inch-long parallel lines lengthwise along the top ¾ inches from either side of the center mark. Place the compass at the end of one line and trace a half circle to join it to the end of the other line. Repeat on the other side to mark a handle hole large enough for your fingers to slip through.

3. Drill a starter hole with a ½-inch drill bit inside the marked hand hole. Use a jigsaw to cut out the handle hole. Use a palm sander or sandpaper to sand top and use a drum sander or sandpaper around sides of handle hole to smooth. If you have a router, router all sides of top with a round-over bit. Otherwise sand all sides with sandpaper. Wipe off dust with tack cloth.

4. Rip one 24-inch-long 1x12 to 11 inches wide, then cross-cut this piece into two 11x12-inch pieces, which will serve as the stool's side pieces. Bevel the table saw blade to 10 degrees, set the fence to cut to 11¼ inches and bevel both top and bottom of one side piece so beveled edges slant in same direction. Repeat for other side piece.

5. Using a compass, draw a 5-inch-diameter semicircle at the center of the bottom edge of both side pieces and cut out with a jigsaw. Use a drum sander or sandpaper to smooth.

6. To attach top to side pieces, measure and mark a line crosswise along the top and underside of the top piece 4" from each short edge. Measure and mark two points along each line about 2 inches from each long edge. Center the top edge of one side piece along one line, then pre-drill two holes at these marks with a 1/16-inch drill bit through the top at an angle into the beveled side piece, making sure side piece is flush with top. Use a drill driver with appropriate bit to countersink the heads of two flathead screws through the top and into the side piece. Repeat for the other side. Hold pieces firmly while attaching screws.

7. Rip one 24-inch-long piece of 1x12 into two 3½-inch-wide pieces called stretchers. Place them in front of the side pieces about 4 inches below and parallel to the top. Mark the cut length, angling side edges in alignment with inside edges of both sides. Set the miter gauge on table saw to 10 degrees and angle cut ends of both pieces to fit within side legs. (Alternatively, you can place stretchers flat against the side pieces just beneath top. If so, measure and mark cut length of stretchers from the inside so they align with the outside angled edges of the side pieces and cut accordingly. The top edge of each stretcher should fit flush beneath the top.)

8. To attach stretchers to finished stool, pre-drill, then countersink screw heads to just past flush with wood.

9. Using a putty knife, fill screw holes with wood filler and scrape smooth. Let dry. Sand all surfaces and edges. Wipe off dust.

10. Apply two coats of primer to entire stepstool, letting dry between coats. Apply two or more coats of paint to entire stool, letting dry between coats. Apply one coat of polyurethane. Let dry.

chic pouf

skill level: intermediate

MATERIALS

- 1-inch-thick foam (we used Poly-fil NU-Foam from Fairfield Processing)
- cylindrical wooden basket (such as wastebasket) with wood rims
- air-soluble fabric marker
- scissors
- tape measure
- heavyweight upholstery fabric
- spray adhesive
- decorative upholstery nails in assorted sizes
- plastic-tipped hammer (we used Osborne No. 36 Fancy Nail Hammer)
- staple gun or glue
- cardboard (optional)

Covered in durable fabric, a compact drum-shaped wooden wastebasket becomes a stylish footstool. For a decorative flourish, hammer a band of brass upholstery nails around the top and upper and lower edges of the barrel. The nailheads' octagonal shape strikes a stylish note, as does the stacked design along the top.

DIRECTIONS

1. Unroll foam to single layer. Trace bottom of basket onto foam; subtract thickness of wood rim from circle all around and cut foam for top of stool. **(NOTE: Bottom of basket is top of stool.)**

2. Measure basket height; subtract height of both wood rims. Measure basket circumference. Cut foam to these dimensions for side.

3. Measure, mark and cut fabric circle 3 inches larger all around than top foam for top cover. Mark and cut fabric 2 inches larger all around than side foam for side cover.

4. Spray one side of foam top with adhesive; smooth onto bottom of basket, leaving wood rim exposed.

5. Spray side piece of foam with adhesive; smooth around center of basket, leaving wood rims exposed.

6. Work with basket bottom-side up. Spray wrong side of top cover with adhesive; smooth onto top of stool so fabric extends evenly on all sides. Pull opposite sides taut and press to rims. Rotate basket a quarter turn; pull opposite sides taut and press to rims. Pull and press remaining edges, always pulling opposite sides as you work to keep fabric taut. Smooth any wrinkles along edges, folding excess fabric into pleats.

7. Spray adhesive along wrong side of one long edge of side cover and turn under 2 inches to form hem. Align this edge of fabric, right side out, along upper edge of stool, covering edges of top cover. Hammer upholstery nail through fabric into upper rim about 2 inches from raw short side edge of fabric.

8. Smooth short side edge of fabric straight down to bottom of stool; hammer upholstery nail through fabric into lower rim about 2 inches from raw short side edge of fabric. Fabric will extend past bottom of stool.

9. At upper edge of stool, pull side fabric taut and even with upper edge of stool; hammer upholstery nail through fabric to upper rim about 1 inch away from first nail. Smooth fabric down; hammer nail through fabric to lower rim about 1 inch from first nail.

10. Continue pulling and nailing fabric around side of stool in same manner, stopping about 2 inches from end.

11. Just before coming full circle, turn under remaining raw short edge of fabric; wrap it over starting edge to test overlap. Adjust as needed to cleanly overlap raw short edge. Trim edge so folded hem is 1 inch deep and overlaps raw edge by at least 1 inch; unfold folded end, spray edge of wrong side of fabric edge with adhesive; press to form hem. Nail folded end to upper and lower edges.

12. Hammer another row of nails just below upper row of nails, and along upper rim edge.

13. Turn stool over. Pull fabric to inside edge; staple or glue about ½ inch from rim on inside. Trim excess fabric. Trace bottom of stool on cardboard, cut out and staple or glue to bottom of stool to finish.

painted demilune table

skill level: beginner

MATERIALS

- old wooden table
- sandpaper
- tack cloth
- paintbrushes
- wood primer
- white acrylic spray paint
- blue acrylic paint
- paint roller
- clear faux-finish glaze
- paint dragging brush for faux finishes
- satin-finish polyurethane sealer

DIRECTIONS

1. Sand all wood surfaces to remove old finish; remove dust with tack cloth.

2. Coat table with primer; let dry. Apply several coats of white paint to table, keeping spray can moving as you work to prevent drips and letting paint dry after each coat.

3. Paint tabletop blue; let dry.

4. Using roller, apply glaze to tabletop. While glaze is still wet, drag brush in even strokes along surface from front to back of tabletop. Let dry.

5. Apply an additional coat of glaze; drag brush along surface in same manner, but this time work from one side edge to the other. Let dry.

6. Apply two or more coats of polyurethane to tabletop, letting dry after each coat.

Let a little paint turn a neglected demilune table into a pretty showpiece. Start by painting the entire table white and then add a coat of robin's egg–blue to the top. After the colored coat of paint dries, coat with a glaze and comb in a crisscross linen pattern for a touch of texture.

elegant end table

skill level: beginner

Place a round of painted plywood atop an inexpensive planter to create an elegant end table, perfect for a sitting area or living room. Paint the table pale yellow or cream, then apply a bronze glaze to the bas relief portions of the urn to accentuate the pretty raised designs.

MATERIALS

- resin or cast-iron urn, about 28 to 32 inches high
- 18- to 25-inch round piece of plywood or round table with screw-in legs (legs not used for this project)
- sandpaper
- damp cloth
- light yellow spray paint
- pencil
- hot-glue gun
- metallic bronze glaze
- foam paintbrush

DIRECTIONS

1. Lightly sand urn and tabletop; remove dust with damp cloth.

2. Apply two coats of yellow spray paint to all surfaces of urn and tabletop, letting paint dry after each coat.

3. Place tabletop on urn, centering it. Mark outline of urn on underside of table. Apply glue to edge of urn; place tabletop on urn, using outline as a guide. Press down to make sure top is level; let dry.

4. Using foam brush, apply a light coat of glaze to urn handles and any urn details, and along table edges as desired. Let dry.

tray table

skill level: intermediate

MATERIALS

- shallow wicker basket
- tape measure
- four flea-market stair balusters
- C-clamps
- hand drill with 3/8-inch bit
- ¼-inch dowel, same length as basket
- level
- handsaw
- sandpaper
- tack cloth
- 2-inch-wide strapping ribbon
- scissors
- heavy-duty staple gun

DIRECTIONS

1. Measure width and length dimensions of basket and make note of them.

2. Using two balusters, form X near a central flat section; clamp together so tops of balusters are spaced almost as wide as basket. Clamp remaining balusters together in same manner, matching shape of X.

3. Drill hole through crossed section on each pair of balusters.

4. Leaving clamps in place, slip one end of dowel through each set of holes, so each X forms a pair of legs at ends of dowel, making stand.

5. Place stand upright. Using level and tape measure, mark a level horizontal line across upper end of each leg (marks will be diagonal to legs); cut each leg at mark, forming flat upper surface. Mark and cut lower ends of legs in same manner so stand is even. Sand cut surfaces to smooth and wipe off dust.

6. Cut two pieces of ribbon, each 1 inch longer than basket width. Turn under ½ inch on each end of each ribbon. Staple ribbon ends to tops of each pair of legs (like a travel luggage rack).

7. Place basket on top of stand.

Merge a weathered quartet of staircase balusters with a rattan tray to create a charming tray table. A metal dowel and wide ribbons secured at the tops of the balusters work in tandem to stylishly support the tray like an elegantly crafted table base.

resurfaced side table

skill level: beginner

Perk up a plain table by topping it with wallpaper that complements your decor. Moisten prepasted wallpaper to activate the adhesive, center the pattern over the tabletop, smooth with a wallpaper brush, then let dry. Turn the table upside down and carefully cut the paper along the table's edge with a craft knife. If your wallpaper isn't scrubbable, brush on a coat or two of all-in-one sealer, if desired, to protect the patterned surface.

painted chest

skill level: intermediate

The boxy shape of this flea-market chest is the inspiration for the clean-lined grid pattern that updates it. Paint the chest a chocolate brown hue, let dry. Then tape off the interlocking pattern and apply burnt-red paint between the taped lines and finish your design with a lacquer-look sealer.

MATERIALS

- wooden chest
- sandpaper
- tack cloth
- paintbrushes
- acrylic paints: brown, red
- pencil
- ruler
- 1-inch-wide painter's tape
- craft knife
- polyurethane sealer

DIRECTIONS

1. Remove drawers from chest; remove drawer pulls. Sand entire chest. Wipe off dust with tack cloth. Apply two coats of brown paint to chest and drawers, letting dry after each coat.

2. Replace drawers. Lightly draw a series of overlapping squares and rectangles on chest, centering motifs from top to bottom and side to side.

3. Apply tape to chest, centered over each line and along all edges. Using craft knife, cut through tape at edge of each drawer. Remove drawers.

4. Apply two or more coats of red paint to chest and drawers, letting dry after each coat and removing tape before last coat of paint dries. Also paint drawer pulls red; let dry. Reattach drawer pulls.

5. Apply two or more coats of sealer to chest and drawers, letting dry after each coat.

chic folding screen

skill level: intermediate

MATERIALS

- three 15x66-inch hollow-core doors
- clear plastic ruler
- air-soluble fabric marker
- 1-inch-thick foam (we used Poly-fil NU-Foam from Fairfield Processing)
- craft knife
- spray adhesive
- fusible fabric adhesive (we used Therm O Web Heat'n Bond Ultrahold Iron-on Adhesive)
- iron
- medium-weight cotton fabric
- double-sided craft tape (we used Therm O Web Double-Sided Super Tape)
- 2-inch-wide ribbon
- clear fabric glue
- pencil
- decorative upholstery nails
- plastic-tipped hammer (we used Osborne No. 36 Fancy Nail Hammer)
- four door hinges with screws
- hand drill with assorted bits

Cover plywood panels or hollow-core doors with fabric to create a chic folding screen that's as pretty as it is practical. Start by padding the center of the boards with foam, then wrap the front and back with fabric, affixing it with fusible web. Frame the edges with two layers of ribbon to create a pretty border, securing them at regular intervals with overscale button nailheads for extra polish.

DIRECTIONS

1. Measure, mark and cut three 11x62-inch pieces of foam.

2. Spray adhesive on one side of each foam piece; center foam on door, smoothing from center out.

3. Cut 2-inch-wide strips of fusible adhesive. Place strips, sticky side down, along wood edges around foam; fuse, then peel off backing.

4. Measure, mark and cut three 35x68-inch pieces of fabric. To make each panel, place a door, foam side up, on fabric, placing one long door edge 1 inch from one long fabric edge, letting fabric extend evenly at top and bottom.

5. Wrap the excess fabric over front of door, covering foam. Press fabric flat along one long edge of front and fuse with iron to fusible adhesive, keeping fabric taut. Repeat along other long edge, then fuse short edges pinching excess fabric at corners into diagonal folds. Using double-sided tape, attach long raw edge of bottom side of fabric to side edge of door. Turn under about ½ inch on remaining long edge of fabric; apply tape along folded edge, then press to door edge to cover raw fabric edge.

6. Tape fabric at top and bottom edges of door in same manner, folding in at corners as if wrapping a gift. Press all taped edges with iron to smooth.

7. Cut 2-inch-wide strips of fabric adhesive. Place strips, sticky side down, along panels' edges; fuse, peel off backing.

8. Cut a 14-foot length of ribbon. Starting at one corner, place ribbon on strip; fuse, stopping about 1 inch from corner. Fold ribbon at 45-degree angle to form mitered corner; continue fusing along each edge in same manner. At end, turn under ribbon at 45-degree angle and trim any excess before fusing.

9. Apply dab of fabric glue under each mitered edge to secure.

10. Measure and mark decorative nail placement, placing one mark at each corner and spacing additional marks evenly about 8 inches apart. Use ruler to keep marks aligned in center of ribbon.

11. Use hammer to lightly tap nails flush with panel surface. Repeat steps 1 through 11 to make other panels.

12. Place panels padded side up, with upper edges aligned. Mark hinge placement on both side edges of center panel, placing tops of hinges about 10 to 12 inches from upper and lower edges and marking positions of screw holes with a pencil. Mark corresponding hinge positions on inner side edges of side panels. To make screen fold accordion-style, mark placement so left hinges face upward and right hinges face downward.

13. Drill pilot holes through fabric at each mark. Screw on hinges.

storage bench

skill level: beginner

MATERIALS

- sandpaper
- 2 small matching wooden stepladders
- two 1x4-foot wood boards, about ¾ inch thick
- tack cloth
- acrylic paint
- paintbrush
- hammer and nails
- nail set
- wood filler

DIRECTIONS

1. Sand edges of stepladders and boards. Wipe off dust with tack cloth.

2. Apply two or more coats of paint to ladders and boards; let dry after each coat.

3. Place open ladders side by side as shown in photo (sand leg ends if needed so ladders are level). Place boards on top of ladders so ends extend evenly.

4. Nail boards to ladders. Using nail set, countersink nailheads. Fill holes with wood filler; let dry.

5. Sand wood filler and touch up paint over filler.

If you've got kids, chances are you've got a messy entry hall. The solution? Build a simple entry bench from a pair of cut-off stepladders and give it a jolt of color. It's a great place for kids to drop off gear or stow schoolbooks. Top its shelves with baskets for scarves, mittens and gloves.

hip headboard

skill level: beginner

A hip headboard will make your bed. Cut a piece of plywood to fit your bed frame and cover it with a grid of circle stickers. Brush an eye-opening shade of orange over the top and add a matching circle-stitched coverlet to tie it all together.

NOTE: If you don't have a headboard, it's easy to make a basic one! Measure from the desired height to the floor, and measure the desired width. Cut a piece of ¾-inch or 1-inch wood board to these measurements.

MATERIALS

- wooden headboard (see Note)
- sandpaper
- tack cloth
- adhesive packaging dots, about 3 inches across
- pencil
- yardstick
- scissors
- foam paintbrush
- rust-colored latex paint
- polyurethane sealer

DIRECTIONS

1. Sand headboard. Wipe off dust with tack cloth.

2. Arrange dots on front of board in desired pattern; we arranged ours in straight rows, evenly spaced. Use a pencil and yardstick to ensure rows and columns are straight, then lightly outline each dot.

3. Cut a small X in center of each dot. Peel backing off one dot at a time; cut backing into 2-inch circle and place on adhesive side of dot, then place dot on board where marked. (Placing this small circle of backing on each dot will allow you to remove it more easily later.)

4. Adhere remaining dots to board where marked.

5. Apply several coats of paint to the headboard, letting dry after all but last coat. Remove dots before last coat of paint dries.

6. Apply several coats of polyurethane to all surfaces, letting dry after each coat.

soft touches

For a quick change of scene or a seasonal update, a fresh swath of fabric can work wonders. Even a little bit can go a long way—a yard of fabric is enough to make up to four new cushion covers, reupholster a footstool or create a tablecloth for a small bistro table. And sewing skills aren't always required. A pair of pretty table napkins can be converted into cute cafe curtains just by attaching clip-on curtain rings and slipping them onto a tension rod. And non-fraying fabrics like felt can be pieced into appealing soft furnishings with just a pair of scissors, some hot glue and a little imagination.

hand-painted pillows

skill level: beginner

MATERIALS

- yellow cotton or linen pillow sham in desired size
- lightweight cardboard 1 inch smaller than sham all around
- adhesive packaging dots, about 3 inches across
- scissors
- ½-inch-wide painter's tape
- foam paintbrush
- Plaid FolkArt acrylic paint in White
- pillow form to fit sham

DIRECTIONS

1. Insert cardboard into sham to prevent paint from seeping through.

2. Cut a small X in center of three dots. Peel backing off one dot at a time; cut backing into 2-inch circle and place on adhesive side of dot, then place dot in center front of sham. (Placing this small circle of backing on the dot will allow you to remove it more easily later.)

3. Adhere two more dots to front of sham, spacing dots evenly.

4. Adhere a strip of tape through centers of circles, then adhere additional strips of tape about 1 inch from circles on each side.

5. Pounce brush in paint, then over dots, working from edges toward center of each section. Remove dots and tape; let dry.

6. Remove cardboard; insert pillow form into sham.

All that's needed to craft your own custom pillows is a little imagination and fabric paint. Choose a limited color palette and pair contemporary motifs with familiar ones for a look that's harmonious, fresh and inviting.

fun felt cushions

skill level: beginner

MATERIALS FOR FLORAL PILLOW

- purchased fabric-covered pillow
- 8½x11-inch sheets of felt in lime green and several shades of blue
- paper-backed fusible web
- iron and ironing board
- pencil
- scissors

MATERIALS FOR PEBBLE PILLOW

- ¾ yard of blue felt
- yardstick
- scissors
- pins
- ¼ yard of turquoise felt
- paper-backed fusible web
- iron and ironing board
- pencil
- scissors
- pins
- blue thread
- sewing machine
- 12x16-inch rectangular pillow form

Feel-good felt is a durable fabric for sewing all-season pillows and also provides a no-sew way to put your own stamp on purchased ones. Borrow shapes from nature, like spa-esque pebbles and lollipop flowers that work organically with any decor. Cut pebbles and stems freestyle; fold small felt circles in half and cut out a semicircle to make the flowers.

FLORAL PILLOW DIRECTIONS

1. Remove insert from pillow.

2. Using iron and following manufacturer's directions, fuse web onto back of each felt piece.

3. Draw stem and circle shapes onto paper side of web; cut out.

4. Fold each circle in half and cut out centers to form rings for flowers.

5. Peel backing off web and arrange flowers and stems as desired on pillow front; trim some flower stems so flowers are at different heights.

6. Use iron to fuse flowers and stems to pillow; replace insert in pillow.

PEBBLE PILLOW DIRECTIONS

1. From blue felt, cut one 13x17-inch piece for pillow front and two 13x10-inch pieces for pillow back.

2. Overlap long edges of back sections to form 13x17-inch rectangle; pin edges.

3. Using iron and following manufacturer's directions, fuse web onto back of turquoise felt. Draw 64 freehand circles, each about 2 inches in diameter, onto paper side of web; cut out.

4. Peel backing off web and arrange circles in tight rows on pillow front, keeping circles away from outer ½ inch of front. Fuse in place.

5. With right sides facing and raw edges even, pin pillow front to back. Sew around edges with ½-inch seams; trim corners and turn right side out.

6. Insert pillow form through opening in back.

cozy dog bed

skill level: intermediate

MATERIALS

- extra-large men's cable-knit sweater (contrasting cuffs, optional)
- yardstick
- chalk marking pencil
- pins
- matching thread
- sewing machine
- scissors
- crib-size quilt batting or loose Poly-fil
- yarn to match sweater
- tapestry needle
- large rectangular or round pillow form

A cozy dog bed wraps your best friend in a snug hug. Stuff a removable pillow into the body of the sweater to form the bed, letting baby bunting–filled arms encircle the sides.

DIRECTIONS

1. Turn sweater inside out. Using yardstick as straightedge, mark a chalk line across top of sweater from shoulder to shoulder front and back; pin front and back together and stitch along line. Cut off excess sweater above line, leaving ½-inch allowance. Remove pins.

2. Using yardstick as straightedge, mark a chalk line across front and back of sweater from armpit to armpit. Pin front and back together and sew along line, forming a tube from one cuff across the chest of the sweater to the other cuff. Remove pins and turn right side out to form side edge of dog bed.

3. Measure length of tube from end to end and divide by 2. Cut 2 pieces of batting to this length, using full width of batting for each piece. Tightly roll each piece of batting and stuff into arms. Alternatively, you may use loose Poly-fil to evenly fill tube.

4. Slip one cuff into the other. Using yarn that matches cuffs and tapestry needle, sew cuffs together to form ring.

5. Slip pillow form into body of sweater. Test pillow size by wrapping side ring around outer edge; add batting remnants around edges if needed to fill out sweater. If sweater is too large, trim excess. Mark around perimeter of pillow insert along top and bottom of sweater with chalk, leaving ½-inch allowance. Remove pillow, cut along lines, pin and sew top and bottom together, leaving a 9-inch opening along one side. Insert pillow form and slipstitch opening closed with yarn.

6. Wrap side ring around pillow; using yarn, whipstitch arms to pillow at lower edge.

pocket pillows

skill level: beginner

MATERIALS

- pillow forms in desired sizes
- tape measure
- chalk marking pencil
- knit or crochet sweaters
- scissors
- matching thread
- sewing machine
- pins
- hand sewing needle

Pocket pillows are as handy as they are comfy with a clever catchall that keeps books and glasses within ready reach. Mix companionable shades of cable and ribbed knits to create a quiet spot to chill.

DIRECTIONS

1. Measure pillow form and add 1 inch to each measurement.

2. Measure, mark and cut two pieces of sweater material to these measurements for pillow front and back.

3. If desired, make a pocket by measuring desired size of pocket; add 1 inch to each measurement. Cut contrasting piece of sweater material to these measurements.

4. Sew zigzag stitches close to cut edges of all pieces.

5. Turn under ½ inch on each edge of pocket; straight-stitch close to edges to hem pocket.

6. Pin pocket to pillow front; stitch close to sides and lower edge.

7. Pin pillow front to back, with right sides facing and raw edges even; stitch edges in ½-inch seams, leaving an 8-inch opening along one edge. Turn right side out.

8. Insert pillow form into cover; slipstitch opening closed.

easy chair coverup

skill level: beginner

MATERIALS

- two striped cotton dishtowels
- flea-market chair
- pins
- matching thread
- sewing machine
- scissors
- iron and ironing board
- chalk marking pencil
- tape measure
- 1¼ yards of 2-inch-wide matching ribbon

DIRECTIONS

1. Drape one towel, wrong side up, crosswise over the seat of the chair, placing one long edge of the towel even with the back of the chair with the short ends extending evenly over the sides and the opposite long edge draping over the front.

2. At each front corner, pull towel front and sides out diagonally to form mitered corner; pin to fit chair snugly (the sides may extend longer than front section).

3. Remove towel from chair and stitch along each pinned corner. Trim seam allowances to ½ inch.

4. If sides are longer than front, turn them under to match length; press edge. Trim pressed edge 1 inch past fold. Turn under ½ inch on raw edge so raw edge meets fold; topstitch to secure hem and complete seat cover.

5. With wrong sides facing and hems even, pin short edge of remaining towel to back edge of seat cover, centering it. Stitch along pinned edge with ½-inch seam; press seam toward second towel.

6. Place cover on seat and drape second towel over back of seat. Mark tie placement on both sides of second towel, placing first set of marks 4 inches from top of seat back and remaining set of marks near lower edge of second towel. Remove cover from seat.

7. Cut ribbon into eight equal pieces. Sew a piece of ribbon under each mark with the raw edges of the ribbon against the wrong side of the towel.

8. Place cover on seat and tie ribbon pairs together to attach slipcover to chair.

Just a few quick stitches convert a pair of striped dishtowels into a chair coverup for a less-than-perfect dining chair. The towels' prefinished edges make them easy to work with for beginners.

decorative duvet cover

skill level: beginner

MATERIALS

- duvet (size depends on your bed)
- tape measure or yardstick
- fabric curtain panel with buttonholes at top
- fabric for reverse side and contrasting border
- air soluable marking pen
- scissors
- pins
- thread
- sewing machine
- iron and ironing board
- buttons
- hand sewing needle

DIRECTIONS FOR EUROPEAN PILLOW SHAMS

1. Measure, mark and cut two pieces of fabric the same size as the pillow forms, plus 1 inch for seam allowance.

2. Pin the pieces together, right sides facing, raw edges matching, and stitch all around, leaving ½-inch seam allowances and a 12-inch opening on one side. Clip the corners of the seam allowances and turn the cover right side out; press.

3. Insert the pillow form or fiberfill. Pin the opening and stitch by machine or by hand, using a slipstitch to close.

Brighten up your bed with a decorative duvet cover made from a shower curtain "framed" in contrasting panels. Make coordinating pillow shams from complementary fabric.

DIRECTIONS

1. For the front: Place duvet on work surface; measure and note its dimensions. Center curtain over duvet, with buttonhole edge 1 inch beyond top. (**NOTE: If your curtain has grommets instead of buttonholes, remove grommets with pliers and hand- or machine-stitch buttonholes.**) Measure the dimensions of any difference on each side and along the bottom, add 1 inch all measurements, and record these dimensions.

2. Measure, mark and cut border panels to these dimensions. Place border panels along side and bottom edges of curtain panel, right sides facing, edges aligned. Fold the corners of the side and bottom border panels to form mitered angles, pin and trim excess. Stitch the mitered corners of the border with ½-inch seams.

3. Place the border back over the curtain panel, top sides facing, raw edges aligned; pin in place. Stitch border to curtain with ½-inch seam allowances.

4. For the back: Measure, mark and cut two widths of fabric to cover the dimensions of the duvet, adding 1½ inches to length, plus an extra 1 inch all around for seam allowances.

5. Turn over and press the top edge with 1-inch double hem. Topstitch in place.

6. With top sides facing and raw edges matching, pin the front and back together and stitch sides and bottom together, leaving ½-inch seam allowances.

7. Turn right side out and press flat. Mark positions of buttonholes on top edge of back cover; hand-sew buttons in place. Insert duvet and button to close.

simple table slipcover

skill level: beginner

A simple slipcover turns a utilitarian shelf into a modern
end table. Organize office or craft supplies in stationery
boxes, mugs and upright files, and cloak with a slipcover
to carve out a now-you-see-it-now-you-don't niche; drop
the top and your work space becomes living space.

NOTE: This project was glued, but you can sew it if you wish. Use a ½-inch seam allowance wherever pieces are glued, and stitch a 1-inch double hem in place.

DIRECTIONS

1. Measure length and width of top of shelf unit or table; add 1 inch to each measurement. Measure, mark and cut piece of fabric to these measurements for cover top.

2. Measure circumference of shelf unit; add 1 inch. Measure height of shelf unit; add 2½ inches. Cut one piece of fabric to these measurements for cover sides.

3. With right sides facing, raw edges matching, glue short ends of side piece of fabric together with ½-inch seam.

4. Turn under and press ½ inch on one long edge of side piece of fabric. Glue pressed edge to outer edges of top piece, raw edges matching.

5. Turn under and press 1 inch double hem along lower edge of side piece; press. Glue in place to hem.

6. Place cover over shelves.

felt ottoman cover

skill level: beginner

MATERIALS

- purchased ottoman (the one shown here is 18 inches square)
- yardstick
- chalk marking pencil
- heavy felt
- scissors
- pins
- matching or contrasting yarn
- tapestry needle

DIRECTIONS

1. Measure top (width and length) and sides (height and width) of ottoman. Cut a piece of felt to each measurement (5 pieces total).

2. Place top piece of felt on ottoman; pin one side piece to edge of top. Using yarn and tapestry needle, make blanket or overcast stitches to join side to top.

3. Attach another side in same manner, then join sides together in same manner, stitching from top to bottom and keeping raw edges even.

4. Continue pinning and stitching sections together to complete cover.

5. Trim lower edges even if needed.

A simple slipcover lets you give an ottoman a seasonal update. Cut five squares of felt to fit an inexpensive cube stool and blanket-stitch them together, starting from the top. Tag-team two ottomans to make a contemporary covered coffee table.

french press cozy

skill level: beginner

MATERIALS

- tape measure
- cable-knit sweater or scarf
- scissors
- contrasting knit sweater or scarf
- pins
- matching threads
- sewing machine with zigzag stitch
- 3 large buttons

DIRECTIONS

1. Measure height and circumference of coffee pot, not including handle; cut a piece of sweater or scarf to these measurements for cover piece, using most interesting part of cable.

2. Cut a strip of contrasting sweater 1 inch wide by same height as pot. With right sides facing and raw edges even, pin and stitch strip to one edge of cover with ¼-inch seam. Turn strip to inside, leaving about ½ inch facing front; sew raw edge to inside of cozy, stitching in the ditch.

3. Sew zigzag stitches along 3 remaining raw edges of cover; turn under ¼ inch on stitched edges and sew again with straight stitch to hem cozy.

4. Measure buttons; make 3 buttonholes, evenly spaced, near trimmed edge of cozy.

5. Sew buttons to opposite edge of cozy; stretch cozy around pot (over handle) and fasten buttons. Cut cozy along handle, making a hole large enough for handle to fit through.

6. Remove cozy; sew zigzag stitches close to edges of handle opening.

The English tea cozy gets a French twist. Cut a rectangle from a cable knit scarf or sweater, stitch the top and bottom to prevent raveling and sew a strip of colored knit to one end. Buttonhole slits for the handle, add buttons and voilà—your own French press cozy.

two-toned button shade

skill level: beginner

MATERIALS

- measuring tape
- 2 contrasting fabrics, for front and back of shade
- scissors
- metal ruler
- pencil
- pins
- twill tape
- thread
- sewing machine
- iron and ironing board
- seam ripper
- 6 buttons
- hand-sewing needle
- tension rod to fit inside window

DIRECTIONS

1. Measure inside of window frame. Measure, mark and cut one piece of each fabric to thee dimensions. Place fabric pieces together, right sides facing, raw edges matching; pin side edges.

2. Cut 3 pieces of twill tape for loops to fit comfortably around buttons, adding an inch for seam allowance.

3. Fold twill tape pieces in half and insert between bottom edge of fabric layer, raw edges aligned. Place one loop ½ inch from each side edge and one in the center. Pin and machine-baste loops in place ¼ inch from raw edges.

4. Sew fabric pieces together, leaving ½-inch seam allowances and an 8-inch opening along the top edge for turning.

5. Turn shade right side out. Draw out loops and press.

6. To create curtain rod channel, topstitch along top of shade 1/8 inch from edge. Topstitch another row of stitching across the shade 1½ inches from the first. Open side seams between channel with a seam ripper.

7. Place two rows of buttons—three at the top and three halfway down the shade—in alignment with the loops, and hand-sew in place.

8. Thread the rod through the channel and mount into window frame.

Give a window privacy and panache with a two-toned button shade. Sew two pieces of fabric together, adding button loops to the bottom, a row of buttons along the top and another row halfway down. Loop the shade up to let in light.

trimmed roman shade

skill level: intermediate

MATERIALS

- tape measure
- chalk marking pencil
- medium-weight damask fabric
- lining fabric
- scissors
- pins
- thread
- sewing machine
- iron and ironing board
- curtain ring tape
- ½-inch-wide fusible hem tape
- hand sewing needle
- 2-inch-long beaded trim
- self-adhesive hook-and-loop tape
- 15 1-inch wood, cut ½ inch shorter than inner width of window
- 3 screw eyes
- shade cord or thin cotton cord
- drill
- 2-inch screws
- ½-inch wood dowel, cut 1 inch shorter than inner width of window
- cord pull
- cleat and screws

An unfussy shade-on-shade ensemble is a space-saving choice for a compact neoclassical bedroom, with contrasting textures, styles and materials. Underneath the damask fabric, a translucent roller shade of natural materials makes a stay-put backdrop for casual accents that "weight" the treatment and lead the eye upward.

DIRECTIONS

1. Measure inside width of window; add ½ inch. Measure inside length of window; add 4 inches. Cut fabric and lining to these measurements.

2. Pin fabric to lining, with right sides facing and raw edges even. Sew sides and lower edge with ½-inch seams. Trim corners; turn right side out. Press. Turn upper raw edges in ½ inch; press and topstitch closed.

3. Turn lower edge up 2 inches; press. Cut three pieces of ring tape, each as long as finished shade, making sure 2 inches of tape extend below the first ring on each piece. Cut three pieces of fusible hem tape to this length.

4. Measure and mark ring tape placement as follows: Mark three lines along the length of the shade: two about 1 inch from each long edge and one down the center. Center fusible hem tape, then ring tape, over each line, positioning bottom rings 1 inch above the top of the hemline, sandwiching tape under the pressed hem. Rings should align on all three pieces. Fuse in place.

5. For extra strength, hand-stitch top of each ring through lining and face fabric.

6. Hand-stitch or machine hem-stitch lower hem in place. Hand-stitch beaded trim to bottom edge of shade, turning ends under ½ inch.

7. Cut hook-and-loop tape to shade width. Separate sections; attach loop section to lining side of upper edge of shade. Attach hook section to one long edge of wood.

8. Attach screw eyes to opposite long edge of wood, spacing them in alignment with rings on shade.

9. Cut three pieces of cord, each twice as long as window length. Tie a cord to bottom ring in one row, then slip cord up through each ring in sequence. Tie and thread cord through each row of rings in same manner.

10. Press hook-and-loop tape sections together to attach shade to wood with screw eyes facing down. Slip each cord through screw eye directly above it.

11. Determine which side of window you wish cords to hang. Slip opposite and center cord through other rings across top so all cords hang on this side.

12. Drill four holes, evenly spaced, through wood piece and top of shade between screw eyes, and screw wood to top of window frame.

13. Slip cord ends through pull; knot about halfway down window. Trim excess cord.

14. Screw cleat to wall about halfway down window. Pull cords to raise shade to desired height; wrap around cleat.

flat panels with contrasting bands

skill level: beginner

Layering fabrics is one of the best ways to get texture and style. Flat panels with contrasting bands of orange patterned silk are combined with chrome rings and finials that echo the hardware on a nearby dresser's drawers, the silk's swirl motif evoking an Asian sensibility.

MATERIALS

- curtain rod and mounting hardware
- tape measure
- chalk marking pencil
- curtain fabric in two coordinating colors
- scissors
- pins
- matching thread
- sewing machine
- iron and ironing board
- hand-sewing needle
- heavyweight non-woven interfacing
- sew-on curtain rings (to match rod)

DIRECTIONS

1. Mount rod above window.

2. Measure the window width and multiply by 2½; divide this figure in half to determine cutting width of each panel. Starting just below the rod, measure the desired finished length of upper section of curtains and add 5 inches to this figure to determine the cutting length. Measure, mark and cut two pieces of one of the fabrics to these measurements. Measure the desired length of lower section of curtain; double this measurement and add 1 inch for cutting length of each lower section. Measure, mark and cut two pieces of the second fabric using the cutting width of the upper curtain panels and the lower section cutting length.

3. With right sides facing and raw edges even, pin the width of one edge of each lower section to the width of one edge of each upper section. Stitch with ½-inch seams. Remove pins and press seam allowances toward lower section.

4. Turn under and press side edges of each panel ½ inch, then 2 inches; pin, then topstitch side hems in place.

5. Turn under and press bottom raw edge of width of each lower section ½ inch. Fold these pressed edges toward wrong side of panels and pin folded edge over seam lines. Pin side edges together, too. Press. Hand-stitch folded bottom edge in place using a hem stitch, then whipstitch the sides closed to finish each two-tone panel.

6. Turn under and press upper edge of each panel ½ inch, then 4 inches. Cut a 4-inch-wide strip of interfacing to finished width of each panel. Open out hem. Place interfacing inside fold lines, aligning ends. Trim ¼ inch from each short end of interfacing. Pin hem to cover interfacing, then topstitch in place.

7. Mark ring placement along upper edge of each panel, placing a ring at each end and spacing remaining rings evenly, about 6 to 8 inches apart. Hand-stitch a ring at each mark.

8. Slip rings onto rod, then mount the rod on the supporting hardware.

surface treatments

When a room needs a redo, few decorating tools do the trick more quickly or effectively than paint. Brighten a wall with a brand-new color or freshen an old floor with stenciled motifs. Certain painted patterns—like bold stripes—are easy to create with little more than a roller and painter's tape. Wallpaper is another great way to add a pop of pattern as well as personality. Even small touches—a shot of vibrant color on the back of a bookshelf or the surprise of floral wallpaper lining the inside of a linen closet—will catch the eye and stoke the imagination.

crown molding picture rail

skill level: intermediate

MATERIALS

- tape measure
- level
- metal yardstick
- pencil
- chalk line
- stud finder
- narrow molding
- miter box and hand saw
- rasp or sanding block
- 6-inch and 1½-inch putty knives

- joint compound
- air nailer or hammer
- 8d finishing nails
- countersink
- sponge
- 150-grit sandpaper
- painter's tape
- primer and paint
- angled sash brush

A little molding goes a long way in adding a sense of substance to a room. Here, crown molding was mounted at plate rail height to lend a feeling of intimacy to the tall room and make the sunny yellow walls pop. In addition, flat, fluted molding framing the area above the fireplace highlights the hearth as a centerpiece of the room.

DIRECTIONS

NOTE: Start by measuring the width of each wall that will receive molding and purchase sufficient molding to cover. If your walls aren't level or plumb, rely on other trimmed elements to guide your eye. In this room, molding was placed just above the windows to guide placement.

1. Select the point at which you'd like to install the molding and use a level, metal yardstick and pencil to mark the start of a straight horizontal line around the walls at the inside and outside corners (see Note). Stretch a chalk line between the marks at each corner and snap lines along the wall. Locate studs and mark their locations with a pencil just below the installation line.

2. To cut the molding at an angle for an inside or outside corner, place it in a miter box upside down and braced against the bottom and side of the box, as if it were angled against a ceiling and wall. Using a hand saw, cut the molding at a 45-degree angle. At inside corners, the top part of the molding will be shorter; at outside corners, the bottom part will be shorter.

3. Using a rasp or sanding block, smooth the back of the angled cut to allow the two corners to come together tightly at the face.

4. To install the molding, start by adhering it to the wall with joint compound. Using a 6-inch putty knife, spread a ½-inch bead of joint compound the length of the molding along the top and bottom edges. Spread the compound liberally on each cut end. As the compound sets, support long runs of molding with 8d nails into studs, using an air nailer or hammer.

5. At the corners, match the profiles of the two mitered ends first, then push together tightly and use compound to fill any small gaps between the molding.

6. Along straight runs, push the straight-cut ends together to create a butt joint. On long runs, place an 8d nail through the molding every few feet and at joints to hold it in place. Angle the nails up slightly to hide the holes, and sink them enough to keep them in place.

7. Clean away excess joint compound while it's still wet. Use your finger to smooth out the seams where the molding meets the wall above and below. Use a wet sponge to help wipe away the compound and clean up the face of the molding. Don't remove too much compound or the seams will hollow as it dries.

8. Using a small putty knife, push more compound into butt joints. Pull the knife over each detail of the profile, leaving a little excess compound along the joint. Once dry, the excess can be sanded smooth.

9. After the joint compound dries completely, sand down the excess using 150-grit sandpaper.

10. Mask the walls along the edges of the molding with painter's tape. Using an angled sash brush, prime and paint the molding to match the door and window casings in the room.

easy wainscoting with plate rail

skill level: intermediate

MATERIALS

- tape measure
- level
- metal yardstick
- pencil
- chalk line
- stud finder
- 1x4 boards
- table saw or hand saw
- miter box and hand saw
- rasp or sanding block
- 6-inch and 1½-inch putty knives
- joint compound
- air nailer or hammer
- 8d finishing nails
- countersink
- sponge
- 150-grit sandpaper
- painter's tape
- primer and paint
- angled sash brush
- paint roller

Create the appealing look of wooden wall paneling without the expense. Apply boards to the wall like raised framing, top the framework with another board to form a narrow shelf and paint the woodwork and the wall area between to create the illusion of full-on wainscoting.

DIRECTIONS

1. Select the height to which you'd like the framework to rise. Using a level, metal yardstick and pencil, mark the start of a straight horizontal line around the walls at the inside and outside corners. Stretch a chalk line between the marks at each corner and snap lines along the wall. Locate studs and mark their locations with a pencil just below the installation line.

2. Place baseboard molding along the floor first. Measure and cut boards to desired width. If you need to butt two boards to cover a long run, you can use scarf cuts to minimize the seams between boards. To make a scarf cut, saw the ends of two boards at 45-degree angles that will overlap to form a clean seam, using a table saw or miter box and hand saw. To cut the board at an angle for an inside or outside corner, cut the ends at a 45-degree angle in the same manner.

3. Using a rasp or sanding block, smooth the back of the angled cut to allow the two corners to meet tightly at the face.

4. To install the baseboards, adhere them to the wall with joint compound. Using a 6-inch putty knife, spread a ½-inch bead of joint compound the length of the board along the top and bottom edges. Spread the compound liberally on each cut end.

5. Along straight runs, push the straight-cut or scarf-cut ends together to create a butt joint.

6. As the compound sets, support long runs of board with 8d nails into studs and into the boards every few feet and at joints to hold it in place, using an air nailer or hammer. Angle the nails up slightly to hide the holes, and sink them enough to keep them in place.

7. Clean away excess joint compound while it's still wet. Use your finger to smooth out the seams where the molding meets the wall above and below. Use a wet sponge to help wipe away the compound and clean up the face of the board. Don't remove too much compound or the seams will hollow as it dries.

8. Using a small putty knife, push more compound into butt joints, leaving a little excess compound along the joint. Once dry, the excess can be sanded smooth.

9. After the joint compound dries completely, sand down the excess using 150-grit sandpaper. Install top of framework along the chalk line marked in step 1, and following the process described in steps 2-9.

10. Determine placement of vertical boards of frame and mark positions on wall. Measure and cut boards to fit between baseboard and top of framework. Apply joint compound and use finishing nails to apply vertical members to walls. Clean away and sand excess joint compound as described in steps 7–9.

11. To create shelf, cut boards, following steps 2–6. Attach shelf to top of framework, using air gun and 8d finishing nails. Use joint compound and sand to fill gaps, as described in steps 7–9.

12. Mask the walls along the edges of the framework with painter's tape. Using an angled sash brush and roller, prime and paint the framework and the wall area within with at least two coats of glossy paint, letting dry between coats.

Squares of textured fabric, mounted in a grid
pattern and trimmed with braid and nailheads
along the interstices, lend texture and warmth
to a gracious den. Applying fabric to walls is
a great way to cover damaged surfaces, too.

NOTE: Before applying any fabric to walls,
remove baseboard or crown molding.
After fabric covering has been applied,
reattach molding.

textured fabric wall grid

skill level: advanced

MATERIALS

- tape measure
- T-square, metal yardstick
- chalk marking pencil
- textured fabric
- scissors
- plumb bob
- chalk line
- liquid starch
- paint tray
- paint roller
- braid
- fabric glue
- rubber-tipped mallet
- decorative nailheads
- optional: molding, joint compound, air nailer or hammer, 8d finishing nails, 150-grit sandpaper, primer, paint and angled sash brush

DIRECTIONS

1. Measure the height of your walls between baseboard and crown molding. Divide the height by 4. Using T-square, yardstick and chalk pencil, measure, mark and cut enough fabric squares to cover the width and height of all the walls you plan to cover with fabric. (Squares pictured are 22x22 inches each.) If you have crown and baseboard molding, add an extra ½ inch to height dimensions of top and bottom squares to be covered by molding. Measure above and below windows and doors and cut fabric accordingly, being careful to match edges on both short strips. Pin a numbered tag to each panel as you work to keep the panels in order around the room.

2. Starting in the least prominent corner of the room, measure out along the ceiling from the corner a distance equal to the width of the material, less about ¼ inch. Set the plumb bob at this point and snap a chalk line to mark the edge for the first panel of fabric.

3. Pour liquid starch into a paint tray or shallow pan. Dip paint roller into starch and roll the starch evenly onto the upper portion of the wall at one corner.

4. Apply the top of a square of fabric to the top of the wall, smoothing it flat with your hands or a wallpaper brush. If desired, bend fabric in half to wrap the corners of adjoining walls.

5. Continue applying squares of fabric in this manner, one below the other until you reach the bottom of the wall, carefully abutting seams.

6. Apply a coat of starch to the entire surface of the fabric that is now attached to the wall. Smooth out any wrinkles with your paint roller, hand or wallpaper brush as you do this. Repeat steps 1–6 until the walls are covered.

7. Measure, mark and cut several strips of braid to the height and width of your walls. Cover seams between fabric squares by stretching braid along vertical seams first, using fabric glue to tack into place. Apply braid over horizontal seams in same manner.

8. Using a rubber mallet, nail heads into points where braid crosses at the interstices.

9. Reattach baseboard and crown molding, if necessary. Or apply crown and baseboard molding if desired following instructions on page 55.

striped accent wall

skill level: beginner

MATERIALS

- carpenter's level
- pencil
- ruler
- painter's tape in assorted widths
- foam paintbrushes
- brown interior latex paint

DIRECTIONS

1. Using carpenter's level, lightly draw a pencil line across wall at about eye level.

2. Draw additional lines above and below first line, spacing lines 2 inches to 12 inches apart as desired.

3. Apply tape over each line, using assorted tape widths to create stripes on wall.

4. Paint bands between lines of tape, starting at tape edges and working toward center of each band. Apply several coats of paint if needed. Remove tape; let dry.

5. Use a smaller paintbrush to touch up edges, if needed.

A can of cocoa-colored paint, a level and painter's tape turn a blah white wall into a look-at-me accent. Give classic stripes an unexpected spin: Space random-width horizontal stripes at varied intervals to entice the eye up a stairwell.

brown bookcases

skill level: beginner

The sharp contrast between the chocolate brown back wall and white-painted book shelves lends drama and richness to a modern room. The brown hue is an easy-on-the-eye neutral that echoes the flooring, but you could paint the back wall any color at all.

painted floorcloth

skill level: beginner

Add a splash of color and personality to a room with a handpainted canvas floorcloth. Large swaths of canvas are readily available at art supply stores, and stamps in a variety of motifs can be found at crafts stores.

MATERIALS

- floorcloth canvas (we cut ours to 4x6 feet)
- yardstick
- pencil
- scissors
- paintbrushes
- acrylic paint in three colors (we used Old Linen and Melon Green from Pratt & Lambert and Crushed Ice from Behr)
- iron and ironing board
- tacky glue
- painter's tape
- one large wall stamp
- polyurethane

DIRECTIONS

1. Measure, mark and cut floorcloth to desired size and apply a base coat of the background color. Let dry completely.

2. Fold under all edges 1 inch to back side; press. Clip off corners on diagonal just above folds to miter; secure edges with tacky glue to hem.

3. Using a yardstick and pencil, measure and mark out grid pattern. Apply painter's tape around edges and over grid pattern. Apply second paint color. Let dry; remove tape.

4. Pour some of the third paint color into a dish, dip stamp into paint, then press stamp onto center of every other square. Let dry.

5. Seal the floorcloth with two coats of polyurethane, letting dry between coats.

painted runner

skill level: beginner

MATERIALS

- woven sisal rug
- pencil
- yardstick
- 2-inch-wide masking tape
- stencil brushes
- Plaid FolkArt acrylic paint in Mustard Yellow

DIRECTIONS

1. Fold rug in half lengthwise; use pencil and yardstick to lightly draw line down center.

2. Draw 2 additional lengthwise lines equally spaced about halfway across the width of the rug along each side of center line.

3. Using tape, mark off crosswise zigzag stripes about 3 inches apart across rug, breaking crosswise lines at each lengthwise line. Also apply tape over rug edges.

4. Using stencil brush, pounce paint between tape lines to make mustard zigzags; remove tape and let dry.

5. Touch up any spots along stripe edges, if needed.

Don't pitch a stained rug—paint it and turn it into fresh floor covering instead. Using a ruler and painter's tape, mark a rickrack pattern on a sisal (or any flat-weave) rug and paint every other row with yellow acrylic paint. No need to get it exactly even. The imperfections actually add to the charm.

hand-painted tile-like motifs

skill level: beginner

Why buy costly custom tile when you can paint something like it for hundreds less? Tape off and paint a 1- to 2-inch border using a standout shade of floor or porch paint. Alternate large round and square medallion stencils to make hand-painted tile-like motifs and seal with polyurethane.

MATERIALS

- tape measure
- pencil
- painter's tape
- paintbrushes
- interior latex paint in rust
- 2 stencils, about 8 inches across
- stencil adhesive
- polyurethane sealer

DIRECTIONS

1. Measure and mark perimeter of portion of floor to be defined with patterns. Mark additional lines about 1½ inches inside this perimeter for border, then apply tape to outer edge of each line.

2. Paint border; remove tape and let dry.

3. Determine placement of stencils within border. Spray back of one stencil with adhesive and position within border. Dip brush in paint, then pounce over stencil, working from edges toward center. Remove stencil before paint dries.

4. Stencil another motif where marked in same manner, rinsing and drying stencil after each use.

5. When all stencils are dry, apply one or more coats of polyurethane over patterned area, letting dry after each coat.

stylish storage

There's no rule that says storage has to be stuffy. Think

beribboned baskets, fabric-covered boxes, even papered

pencil holders. The possibilities expand when you consider

the prospect of repurposing old things for new uses. Imagine

a decorative garden urn as an umbrella holder or a bucket

as a portable toolbox. When splashed with bright color

or covered with a lively patterned paper, even boring bins

can become just as peppy as they are practical.

fabric-covered boxes

skill level: beginner

Decorative fabric-covered boxes hide things in anything-but-plain sight. Working bottom to top, brush the exterior of the box with glue and wrap it in fabric like you would a gift. Trim with ribbon.

MATERIALS (FOR ONE BOX)

- empty box
- enough fabric to cover the top, sides and bottom of box
- scissors
- Mod Podge or other craft glue
- paintbrush
- 2-inch-wide grosgrain ribbon

DIRECTIONS

1. Center the bottom of the box over the back side of the fabric. Trim the fabric so that there is enough to pull up and cover the sides, plus 1 inch.

2. Apply Mod Podge to the bottom of the box with the paintbrush. Place the box onto the back side of the fabric and smooth out any wrinkles.

3. Apply Mod Podge to one of the longer sides of the box; pull up the fabric to cover the side. Apply glue along the top inner edge of the box, fold over the fabric and press in place. Repeat on the other long side.

4. Apply Mod Podge to short sides of box, fold in the fabric as you would with a gift wrap and pull fabric up to cover the short ends. You may trim away excess at fabric corners and fold in raw edges before applying fabric to create a smoother finish if desired. Fold over and glue the raw edges of the fabric to the inside of the box.

5. Repeat Steps 1 through 4 to cover the lid.

6. Cut a 3-inch piece of ribbon and fold in half to form a loop. Glue the loop to the inside edge of the lid, letting loop extend about an inch. Let dry. Cover box with lid.

color-coordinated storage system

skill level: beginner

Create your own color-coordinated storage system by covering a trio of unique decorative boxes with a vibrant mix of wallpapers in the same color family. Or, for a subtler effect, cover boxes in the same style and size with a single pattern.

MATERIALS

- plain lidded boxes in various shapes and sizes
- tape measure
- yardstick
- pencil
- wallpaper (in various patterns if desired)
- straightedge
- craft knife
- cutting mat
- paper towels
- spray glue (optional)

DIRECTIONS

1. Measure and mark the circumference of your box and add –½ inch. Measure the height of your box and add ¾ inch. Measure and mark a rectangle with these dimensions on the back of the wallpaper. Using a straight edge and craft knife, cut out the rectangle.

2. Measure the circumference of your lid and add ½ inch. Measure the height of your lid. Measure and mark a strip to these dimensions on the back side of the wallpaper. Using a straightedge and craft knife, cut out the strip.

3. Center the pattern of the paper on top of the lid, then turn the lid and paper facedown on a cutting mat. Holding the lid firmly in place, trace around the outer edge of the lid onto the back side of the paper. Holding lid in place, use a craft knife to cut along the line of the outer edge of the lid.

4. Following the manufacturer's instructions, soak the wallpaper in water to activate adhesive. Wrap side piece around box, overlapping the ends at the seam and turning the top edge of the paper over to the inside of the box. Use a straightedge to press out bubbles and smooth paper. Use paper towels to wipe off excess adhesive. (If your wallpaper is not prepasted, use spray glue on the back of the paper.) Hold the paper in place until it sets, then let dry. Repeat this process for the side and top of the lid, letting lid dry top down. (If the wallpaper expands, you may need to trim the wallpaper again to fit the lid after it dries.)

hardworking wall shelves

skill level: beginner

MATERIALS

- carpenter's level
- pencil
- wooden or fiberboard shelves or 1x12-inch boards cut to size
- mounting brackets and screws
- acrylic paints: white, red
- paintbrushes
- screwdriver
- assorted fabric-covered desk accessories (such as binders, desk blotter and boxes) in orange and red
- small labels with metal frames
- craft glue

DIRECTIONS

1. Using level, mark shelf placement on wall above desk. Space shelves to allow for size of desk accessories.

2. Paint shelves and brackets white; let dry. Paint tops and edges of shelves red; let dry.

3. Mount brackets on wall where marked; place shelves on brackets.

4. Glue labels to fronts of boxes and spines of binders.

Hardworking wall shelves combine function with flair. Store low-priority items up high in labeled boxes, file papers in easy-to-grab binders and display everyday essentials in cups and baskets—all purchased or painted in shades of energizing orange and red.

papered pencil cups

skill level: beginner

Green up your desk with recycled cans-turned-
pencil-cups. Cover washed-out soup cans and
tea tins with color copies of your favorite photos
or art paper, cut to fit and hot-glued in place.
Fill with pens, scissors and other necessities
to keep conveniently close at hand.

MATERIALS

- tin can
- sandpaper
- tape measure
- pencil
- printed paper, such as gift
  wrap or an enlargement of
  a color photograph
- scissors
- spray adhesive

DIRECTIONS

1. Rinse and dry an empty tin food
can. Sand the upper edge to smooth
interior surface.

2. Measure can circumference; add
½ inch. Measure can height. Measure,
mark and cut a piece of printed paper
to these measurements.

3. Spray adhesive on wrong side of
paper, then smooth onto sides of can,
working from center out to eliminate
air bubbles.

nesting baskets

skill level: beginner

Bathrooms are notoriously space-challenged, but any wall offers triple the storage when you think vertical. Tier woven nesting baskets by looping twine through the corners; knot the top and suspend from a hook to keep toiletries and towels within ready reach.

MATERIALS

- spool of heavy cord or twine
- tape measure
- scissors
- set of three nesting wicker baskets
- slim screwdriver (optional)
- heavy-duty screw-in cup hook

DIRECTIONS

1. Cut four 2-yard lengths of cord. Tie one to each corner of large basket by pushing ends between woven strands. Use a slim screwdriver to nudge the twine through the strands if necessary.

2. Measure up about 12 inches on each cord; tie a small overhand knot. Slip ends through corners of medium basket in same manner, pulling cords until small knots rest on basket rim, then wrap and slip cords back through same holes to secure.

3. Measure 12 inches again and attach small basket in same manner.

4. Screw cup hook to wall at desired height.

5. Loosely tie all cords together near ends and loop over cup hook. Adjust knot so baskets lie flat on wall (front cords will be longer than back; you may need to adjust small corner knots slightly). When correct angle is achieved, tie all cords together near ends. Trim excess cord; hang baskets on hook.

fabric-covered bin

skill level: beginner

MATERIALS

- large plastic storage bin
- tape measure
- handheld drill with bits
- cotton fabric in desired pattern
- chalk marking pencil
- scissors
- iron and ironing board
- decoupage medium
- foam paintbrush
- awl
- heavy twine or rope
- 4 plastic wheels and mounting hardware

Ignored space under seating is a perfect parking spot for stow-it-low bins. Use a glue/sealer, such as Mod Podge, to affix decor-friendly fabric to low-cost plastic bins, then drill holes to attach rope pulls and wheels. Load up the bins with seasonal items, like towels or throws, which can be rolled out and in as needed.

DIRECTIONS

1. Place bin bottom side up. About 1 inch from each corner, drill a hole large enough to accommodate stem of wheel. Place bin right side up. Drill two holes, about 4 inches apart, on front of bin for handle.

2. Measure circumference and height of bin; add 3 inches to each measurement. Measure, mark and cut fabric to these measurements. Fold over one long edge of fabric 1 inch and press.

3. Place bin on work surface with one side up; brush on a generous coat of decoupage medium. Smooth fabric over side, aligning pressed folded edge just under rim of bin and allowing excess to extend at bottom.

4. Rotate bin on work surface with adjacent side up; apply medium and smooth fabric in place in same manner. Continue attaching fabric to each side of bin in same manner.

5. At raw edge, turn fabric under 1 inch and use additional medium to secure lapped edges.

6. Apply medium to outer 2 inches of bin bottom and smooth fabric in place, forming mitered corners.

7. Using awl, puncture fabric over each of the four wheel holes and each of the two handle holes.

8. Cut 10 inches of twine; push twine ends through handle holes and knot on inside, leaving some slack.

9. Attach wheels to each lower corner hole.

wrapping station

skill level: beginner

MATERIALS

- wooden crate (about 12 to 14 inches long)
- metal yardstick
- pencil
- drill with $^3/_8$-inch bit
- sandpaper
- two $^1/_4$-inch wooden dowels, about 2 inches longer than length of box

DIRECTIONS

1. Stand crate on one long side. Mark positions for two dowel holes on each side of crate, centering holes and making sure they're level from side to side.

2. Drill a hole at each mark. Sand crate and dowel ends.

3. Insert each dowel through one hole, then through ribbon spools, then through opposite hole.

Repurposed crates turn a tabletop into a sewing or wrapping station. Slide rolls of ribbon and twine onto wooden dowels that stack double-decker in holes drilled inside a packing crate. Stash notions in glass jars and odds and ends in hatboxes marked with stick-on labels.

pot rack

skill level: intermediate

MATERIALS

- 3-foot-long section of ladder (we used a small ladder, but you can cut a 3-foot section from an old ladder, making sure to include 3 rungs in the section)
- ruler
- pencil
- hand drill and bits
- 8 screw hooks
- stud finder
- 4 toggle bolts
- four 5-foot lengths of heavy-duty chain (ask hardware store for recommended chain weight for this project)
- large pot hooks

Pot racks can add storage and give a ho-hum kitchen the look of a "cook's kitchen," but they can also be expensive. Not a problem when you repurpose an old ladder into a perfect pot rack. A weathered ladder gives this kitchen a rustic touch. For a sleeker look, paint it black, or choose a metal one that complements stainless steel appliances.

DIRECTIONS

1. Measure and mark screw hook placement on ladder, centering marks about 4 inches from each end of ladder. Drill pilot hole at each mark.

2. Screw a hook into each hole.

3. Using stud finder, locate ceiling joists. Mark toggle bolt placement along joists, spacing them the same distance apart as the screw hooks. Attach toggle bolts to joists. Attach a screw hook to each toggle bolt.

4. Attach one end of each chain to each ceiling hook; attach other end of each chain to ladder hooks.

5. Adjust chains if needed so pot rack hangs at desired height, allowing for clearance when pots are hanging from rack.

6. Slip pot hooks over ladder rungs and hang pots.

by-the-door noteboard

skill level: beginner

MATERIALS

- 4x5-foot piece of ½-inch-thick Homasote (see Note)
- spray adhesive
- 2 yards of brown burlap or heavy cotton fabric
- scissors
- heavy-duty stapler
- 2 yards of 2-inch-wide ribbon
- 3 yards of 1-inch-wide ribbon
- 3 Masonite or wooden letters as desired
- chrome spray paint
- 4 printed cotton napkins
- thumbtacks
- carpenter's level
- pencil
- drill with screwdriver bits
- long wood screws
- wall anchors (optional)
- D-rings

NOTE: Homasote is a wallboard made from recycled paper pulp. It can be purchased at home-improvement stores; ask to have it cut to size for you at the store, or use a circular saw or table saw to cut at home.

A noteboard keeps a busy family on track. Staple fabric to a piece of custom-cut Homasote and designate personal spaces with ribbon and letters. Thumbtack on napkin pockets to corral papers and pens, and position a bench to catch grab-and-go items.

DIRECTIONS

1. Spray adhesive on one side of Homasote. Smooth fabric over glue so fabric extends beyond each side; trim excess fabric so that it extends 3 inches beyond edges of board on all sides.

2. Turn board over; fold fabric toward back, tucking in diagonally at corners and stapling to back. Continue stapling fabric to board, spacing staples about 4 to 6 inches apart.

3. Place board faceup on work surface. Place 2-inch-wide ribbon across width of board, about 1 foot from top; fold ends over to back and staple in place.

4. Cut strip of 1-inch-wide ribbon in half; place strips along height of board, evenly spaced to form three equal sections. Fold ends over to back and staple in place.

5. Spray-paint letters; let dry. Glue a letter to each section of board, above wide ribbon.

6. Fold two napkins in half, right sides out, to form pockets. With folded edge down, tack to each side section of board near lower corners (slip papers, envelopes, etc., between fabric layers to hold in place).

7. To make double pocket for center section of board, fold two napkins in half, right sides out. Fold one napkin in half again and place on top of other napkin, with folded edges aligned at bottom. Tack both layers of napkins to center section of board at corners and where shorter napkin ends. Use additional tacks to split pockets into sections, if desired.

8. Use a carpenter's level to mark positions of wood screws for mounting into wall studs if possible. If you can't find studs, mount screws into wall using wall anchors. Attach D-rings to back of message board in alignment with screws; hang D-rings on screws to mount board on wall.

magazine holder

skill level: beginner

MATERIALS

- 1 yard of cream-colored heavyweight linen or burlap fabric
- cast-iron garden urn (see Note)
- hot-glue gun
- scissors

DIRECTIONS

1. Drape fabric over top of urn so it extends evenly on all sides. Push center of fabric into urn so it covers the bottom in a smooth layer.

2. Lifting up small sections at a time, glue center of fabric to urn.

3. Smooth fabric up along sides of urn, forming about 8 pleats as you go. Glue layers together in the middle of each pleat, then glue pleats to urn.

4. When glue dries, trim excess fabric even with upper edge of urn. Turn under ½ inch on upper edge and glue, if desired.

NOTE: Our urn had an antique painted finish, but if yours is plain, use a faux-finish paint kit from the hardware store to give it an aged effect, if desired, before starting the project.

Lined with a remnant of burlap, this antique urn makes a stylish magazine holder, adding character and charm to any home library.

artful collections

Whether it's a trove of vintage teacups, a mass of matchboxes, a stash of stamps or an array of architectural artifacts, nothing grabs the eye or tells a story like collectibles. The trick is to display them with the same care and consideration that it takes to amass them. Cherished pieces deserve a place of their own—and often a prominent one. Conscientious editing is also key. Showing only the best of your bunch—or at least just a select few at any given time—enables the collection to coexist as a harmonious ensemble while giving individual pieces room to shine.

sculptural ceramics

The 19th-century English designer William Morris said, "Have nothing in your house that you do not know to be useful or believe to be beautiful." Display it all together, and it's more beautiful still, adds New Canaan, Connecticut–based designer Ingrid Leess. Her home is filled with useful art—glass and ceramic pieces that are as practical as they are lovely.

And the beauty they add to her home can also be yours for the arranging. Add color to walls without having to paint. Group like objects to lend importance, or mix them up to delight the eye. Fill shelves and cabinets with things you love—and use—and you, too, can bring out both the functional and artistic best in your own collections.

"White is soothing," designer Ingrid Leess says, "especially if a collection is large." She turned an entire wall into a panorama of flea-market finds, hand-thrown ceramics and inexpensive Ikea pieces, unified by organic shapes and a streamlined palette. Painting walls and shelves white and spiking the display with polished wood, the occasional dried blossom, mercury glass and pewter lends points of contrast.

This pared-down vignette is a soft, modern accent to the black side table it adorns. The spiky white artichokes echo the dahlia's petals, and their angular tips point straight to the X of the lantern. Sticking to one color lets the shapes speak for themselves, and the differing heights draw the eye in a circle from one to the other.

eclectic curios

Though some experts say the cardinal rule for collectors is to "buy what you love," flea-market maven Marie Moss warns that there's more to it than that. "It's important to give some thought to function when collecting," she says. "Life's too short to be saving things that you'll never use. Serve your meals on antique dishes, use vintage magazines for craft projects, burn those old candles, and find a new purpose for the things you collect." Of her collection of old wicker and straw handbags, for example, which, displayed as a group on a shelf when not in use, add texture to her bedroom, Marie says, "I take these wherever I go."

Marie uses shelving in the guest room to showcase a few of her favorite finds. She stocks the shelves with kitschy 1950s novels, just like an old bed-and-breakfast would, along with souvenirs and fabric-covered boxes. All of the comfy bedding is vintage. Even her coddled canine, Harriet Dixie, was rescued secondhand from a local shelter.

A collection of old trunks holds a trove of found treasures, including dolls' clothes, photographs and overflow items from other rooms in the house. The unique lamp, its shade blooming with vintage millinery flowers, was purchased at an antique market in Chicago.

Now a resident of suburban Chicago, Marie is a self-described "Jersey girl," born and raised near the New Jersey shore. To fight off homesickness, she gives her large collection of shell crafts, starfish and other seaside mementos prime placement on the table in the foyer. "It's the first thing you see when you walk in," says Marie, "and always makes me smile."

vintage tins

Nothing takes the chill off a cold winter day like a cozy room—a space that welcomes and puts you at ease. It's the room with the comfy loveseat and a place to kick up your feet, the place where toys, hand-me-down furniture and offbeat collectibles commingle. It's where nothing is precious except the good vibes it offers..

A shelf near the ceiling is a perfect
perch for a chocolate-mold collection.

ever-changing displays

Art isn't always captured on canvas or hung on the wall.
Statuesque glass wine vessels in sea greens and blues
become a tabletop still life when filled with willowy
greenery from Leess' yard. Set atop a long table and
grouped with whimsical accents, like a glass fish bottle
and a bull's-eye plate, they give personality to a bare
wall behind a sofa. Lamps hand-fashioned from old glass
bottles make creative and functional endpieces.

Classic blue-and-white is crisp and refreshing, whether you're dining or decorating. Follow Leess' lead and group a collection of pieces that serve both ends. Limit patterns to stripes, polka dots and toile-like florals, allowing a diversity of serving pieces to live in harmony. Store seldom-used items on a soffit or over-the-window shelf, clustering similar pieces together so they read as a collection.

vignettes

Faced with a bare surface, it's tempting to go all or nothing—clutter it with knickknacks or leave it spare. Instead, add carefully selected objects to define the space. Choose a well-edited group of items with something in common, like a shape, motif or color, then build your vignette piece by piece to achieve a harmonious look. The end result: a pleasing scene with decorator polish.

A quartet of artwork with an avian theme in a washed-out garden palette creates a focal point above a pale dresser. Layers of complementary vignettes with related motifs—not just birds, but blossoming branches and harmonious hues—add dimension to the scene. One mini vignette flows seamlessly into the next—just as the branches of floral arrangement reach up to the art, the cloche and the porcelain dove layer in front of the picture frames.

paper remnants

A gorgeous wallpaper—especially one with a large-scale print—can be like a work of art, so why not frame a swatch and display it like one? Or better yet, frame three or more papers in complementary frames of different sizes for a gallery effect.

This funky globe clock is sure to wow when understatement just won't do. Cut six desktop globes in half, bind the edges with bookbinder's tape and hang them floor-to-ceiling around an oversized clock kit spray-painted sea blue. Paint the wall a sunny yellow and watch the world tick by.

easy accents

If God is in the details, then decorative accents are essential

grace notes in a room. The best accents appeal not just to the

eye, but to the other senses as well. Picture the doubly inviting

allure of a soft-to-the-touch embroidered pillow, a shapely

vase filled with fresh-scented flowers, a charming ceramic

dish filled with chocolates, or a whimsical tinkling wind

chime. More than mere eye-candy, meaningful decorative

accents invariably serve useful purposes. And—especially

when crafted by hand—they add indispensable character, too.

cast-resin letters

skill level: beginner

SIZE: 10½" HIGH

MATERIALS

- heavy paper to cover work area
- rubber gloves
- Yaley Enterprises' Deep Flex gallon-size clear casting resin and catalyst (#18-2428)
- graduated paper cups (for measuring) #68-8709
- paper cups for mixing
- eyedropper #110285
- white resin dye #187-6345
- craft sticks

- gel promoter #66-2402
- letter molds J #02-2272, O #02-2277, Y #02-2287 (request that the molds be made in resin plastic)
- resin surface hardener #65-2402
- Hang-a-Plaks, lightweight #77-0012
- fine sandpaper (optional)
- white spray paint (optional)
- clear plastic spray #40-2113
- acetone #17-2416 (for cleanup)

DIRECTIONS

1. Spread heavy paper over your work surface. Read instructions included with Deep Flex casting resin and catalyst before beginning. Wearing rubber gloves, pour approximately 12 ounces of the resin into paper mixing cup (you will have to use more than one cup if using an 8-ounce graduated cup). This resin will be used to make the first of two pours that will be necessary for this project.

2. Using eyedropper, add white opaque resin dye to resin mixture—a few drops per ounce of resin is sufficient. Stir thoroughly.

3. Following manufacturer's instructions, add catalyst to resin mixture. Stir thoroughly.

4. Using eyedropper, add 1 to 4 drops of gel promoter for each ounce of resin to mixture. Stir thoroughly.

5. Pour resin mixture into molds (approximately 4 ounces per letter).

6. Let resin set about 10 to 20 minutes until it gels—the resin will have a rippled appearance on the surface. Gelling times may vary.

7. Measure approximately 24 ounces of resin and pour into mixing cup for your second pour.

8. Using eyedropper, add white opaque resin dye (a few drops per ounce). Stir thoroughly. Add catalyst, according to instructions. Stir thoroughly.

9. Add resin surface hardener at this time to help eliminate the stickiness from the back of your casting if desired. Use 6 drops of hardener per ounce of resin. Stir thoroughly.

10. Pour into molds; wait approximately 20 minutes until resin gels, then insert Hang-a-Plaks. Let set until the finished pieces are hard with no tackiness—approximately 24 hours.

11. Remove the castings from the molds by gently flexing the molds to release the vacuum. If necessary, sand edges until smooth.

12. Spray castings with white spray paint if needed. (This is necessary if the hangers are showing through the white casting.) Spray with topcoat of clear plastic spray.

Handmade cast resin letters add character and dimension to shelves or mantels. Use them to spell out uplifting words or messages to brighten the spirit of a room, or use letters like monograms to personalize bedrooms or private spaces.

art kitchen clock

skill level: beginner

MATERIALS

- wood frame in desired size (you can use an old frame without glass)
- white acrylic paint
- paintbrush
- yardstick
- flea-market wood sign (or decorative wood fruit crate)
- pencil
- handsaw
- hand drill with bits
- clock kit (from crafts store; contains hands and clockworks)
- hot-glue gun

DIRECTIONS

1. If frame has glass and back, remove them (not needed for this project).

2. Apply several coats of white paint to frame, letting dry after each coat. You can use a soft cloth to wipe away some of the paint before it dries for an aged look, if desired.

3. Measure frame opening; mark these dimensions on wood sign, centering the most interesting part of the sign in the measured area.

4. Cut out sign to form clock face.

5. On wrong side of face, mark a line from upper right to lower left corner, then from upper left to lower right corner, forming an X. Refer to clock kit for size of hole required for your kit; drill hole at center of X.

6. Follow kit directions to mount clockworks on back of face and hands on front.

7. Apply glue to outer edges of face; place in frame.

Snipped to fit an inexpensive wood frame, a farmstand sign—salvaged from the side of an old crate—becomes the fresh face of an art kitchen clock. Use a drill to create a hole for the battery-operated clock hands (available in crafts stores).

time zone clocks

skill level: beginner

MATERIALS

- 4 black wooden frames
- metal yardstick
- pencil
- foam-core board
- craft knife
- scissors
- 4 subway maps
- spray adhesive
- tape measure
- large awl
- red spray paint
- 4 clockworks kits
- picture hooks
- hammer

DIRECTIONS

1. Measure, mark and cut four pieces of foam-core board to fit frames.

2. Measure, mark and cut maps to fit tops of each piece of foam-core.

3. Spray backs of maps with adhesive and affix to each board.

4. Measure longest clock hand; add 1 inch. Using this dimension, mark position of hole from one corner of each board; use awl to make hole for clockworks shaft.

5. Spray-paint hands of clockworks red. Follow clockwork manufacturer's directions to attach movements to back of each board and hands to front. Set clocks to time in time zones depicted in maps, if desired.

6. Mount foam-core in frames. Mount frames to wall, using picture hooks.

A quartet of black-framed maps is a colorful commentary on the time zone clocks found in newsrooms from New York to Paris. Use spray adhesive to mount subway maps from different countries on foam-core backs cut to fit store-bought frames. Accent each map with clockworks spray-painted red.

starburst clock

skill level: intermediate

MATERIALS

- papier-mâché boxes, one 3-inch- and six 2-inch-diameter
- ruler
- pencil
- hole punch
- six 12-foot-long, ¼-inch-diameter wood dowels
- wood glue
- acrylic paints: white, plus seven bright colors
- paintbrushes
- clockworks kit (works should be smaller than 3 inches across)

DIRECTIONS

1. Remove box lids (not needed for this project). Around perimeter of large box, make six equally spaced marks ¼ inch from upper edge; punch hole at each mark. On each small box, punch one hole ¼ inch from upper edge.

2. Place all boxes open side down. Glue dowels into holes in large box; glue a small box to end of each dowel.

3. Paint boxes and dowels white; let dry. Paint each box a different bright color; let dry.

4. Follow clockwork manufacturer's directions to attach movement to inside of large box and hands to bottom and mount on wall.

A retro starburst clock gets a mod makeover. Punch six holes around the edge of a round papier-mâché box and connect six smaller boxes to it with ¼-inch wooden dowels. Paint the boxes and clock hands Pop Art colors, then punch the shaft through the center box top and hide the battery inside.

stenciled shade

skill level: beginner

The modern lines of this lamp are stark, but an array of layered classic stencil motifs painted in vibrant give its shade lighthearted flavor.

MATERIALS

- lamp with paper shade
- stencil adhesive
- various stencils
  (we used some from Plaid)
- stencil paint in assorted colors
- paper plates
- stencil brush

DIRECTIONS

1. Remove shade from lamp. Spray back of stencil with adhesive, then position on shade as desired.

2. Pour paint onto plate. Dip brush into paint, then pounce over stencil, starting at edges, working toward center. Hold shade under stencil to keep surface steady. Remove and wash stencil; let paint dry.

3. Spray and reposition stencil on shade, overlapping first image. Pounce over stencil with new color.

4. Continue stenciling images in overlapping layers as desired and repeating process with different stencils and different colors.

beribboned lampshade

skill level: beginner

Using leftover ribbons in various colors, glue equal lengths in a random pattern around a shade, affixing the ends inside at the top and bottom seams. This easy lampshade will have you looking at your decor in a whole new light.

MATERIALS

- flea-market lamp
- shade to fit lamp
- tape measure
- grosgrain ribbon in assorted widths and colors
- scissors
- hot-glue gun

DIRECTIONS

1. Remove old shade from lamp.

2. Measure new shade from top to bottom; add 2 inches. Cut various ribbons into several pieces to this length.

3. Place new shade on lamp (this will help you keep the ribbons straight). Starting with wider ribbon, apply glue to back and place it straight down shade so it extends evenly at top and bottom. Smooth into place, tucking ends to the wrong side of shade at top and bottom.

4. Working around shade, continue to apply ribbons in the same manner. Ribbons may overlap slightly at upper edge, depending on shape of shade. Start with wider ribbons, then use narrow ribbons to cover any overlapping areas.

painted branch base

skill level: beginner

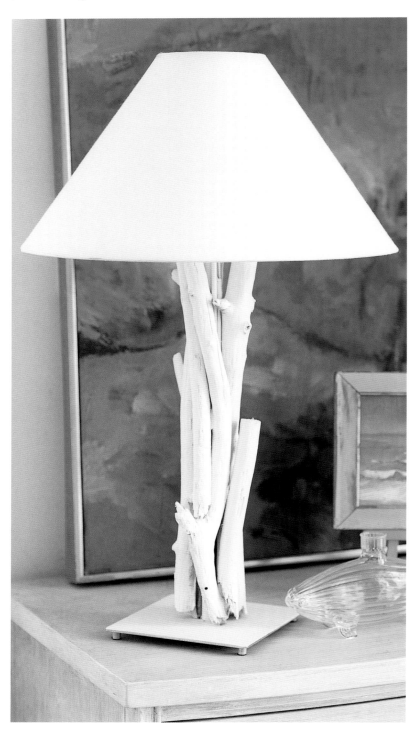

MATERIALS

- dry, fallen tree branches
- saw
- sandpaper
- matte white spray paint
- hot-glue gun
- lamp and shade

DIRECTIONS

1. Cut wood to height of lamp base, varying lengths slightly. Sand cut ends.

2. Clean and dry wood. Apply several thin, even coats of paint to all surfaces of each branch, letting dry after each coat.

3. Glue wood vertically to cover lamp base.

Turn a college-dorm-style lamp into a sculptural centerpiece by covering a spindle base with a tangle of graceful birch branches. The look is fresh and organic.

petal-adorned pendant

skill level: beginner

MATERIALS

- faux lilies
- scissors
- white paper lantern (from party supply store)
- hot-glue gun

DIRECTIONS

1. Cut stems off flowers, cutting as close to base of flower as possible.

2. Starting at center, glue blossoms onto lantern, working in staggered rows around lantern to cover completely.

3. Hang on bulb on pendant cord.

Turn a Chinese paper lantern into a petal-adorned pendant in no time. All you need to complete the flirty makeover is an assortment of faux flowers and a hot-glue gun.

twig mirror

skill level: beginner

MATERIALS

- assorted dry twigs
- garden snips
- green spray paint
- hot-glue gun
- flea-market mirror

DIRECTIONS

1. Cut twigs into 3- to 5-inch pieces, depending upon size of mirror.

2. Place twigs on newspaper; apply several light coats of paint, letting dry and turning twigs over after each coat.

3. Glue twigs to mirror, starting about 2 inches from outer edge (if mirror has frame, be sure to cover frame); apply twigs in overlapping layers as you work toward outer edge. Let dry.

Layers of painted twigs and a hot-glue gun are all you need to recycle a yard-sale mirror into eco-friendly wall art. For best results, be sure the twigs are completely dry before you start.

studded frames

skill level: beginner

Studded frames give the look of custom framing without the price tag. Hammer large and small nailheads around the edges of store-bought frames, creating interest with simple leaf or scroll designs at the corners and centers. Before embellishing them, we painted our frames in twoshades of green and used them to frame pressed leaves.

MATERIALS

- wood picture frame with broad flat surface
- paintbrush
- wood primer
- acrylic paint
- cardboard remnant, same size as frame
- pencil
- clear plastic ruler
- hand drill with very narrow bit
- decorative upholstery nails in assorted sizes
- plastic-tipped hammer (we used Osborne No. 36 Fancy Nail Hammer)
- clear craft glue (optional)

DIRECTIONS

1. Remove glass and backing from frame. Apply two coats of primer to frame; let dry.

2. Apply two coats of paint to frame; let dry after each coat.

3. Test desired nail pattern by drawing on cardboard. Allow at least half of nail's diameter between marks and edges of frame so nails don't hang over edges.

4. Mark frame same as cardboard, using ruler to keep marks aligned.

5. Using bit slightly smaller than nail's point, drill pilot holes at marks.

6. Push nails into holes, then use hammer to lightly tap nails flush with frame surface. If nails are not tight in holes, remove and dab glue on points before reinserting.

foodie art

skill level: beginner

Foodie art makes a focal point few can resist.
Photograph vibrant fruits, vegetables and spices
against a stark backdrop. Finish with crisp white
mats and sleek black frames to create custom art
right from your own kitchen.

MATERIALS

- food items of your choosing to photograph
- piece of beige or off-white linen for photography backdrop
- digital camera with USB cord
- computer with photo program
- 2 white mats to fit your frames (available at crafts stores)
- archival art tape
- 3 black frames in desired sizes

DIRECTIONS

1. Place food on linen and photograph.

2. Download images to your computer via the USB cord using your photo program, and alter photos to your choosing (black-and-white, sepia, etc.).

3. Go to *shutterfly.com* (or any other photo reproduction venue) and upload selected photos to site. Note: Shutterfly is free to join and also offers options to alter colors of images if your photo program does not.

4. Order prints in desired sizes; they take about three to five days to arrive via regular mail.

5. Attach photo prints to matting (if applicable) with tape at top of print only and set in frames.

TIP: The key to the success of these photographs is to take very graphic photos, either straight-on (such as the garlic in pedestal bowl) or from bird's-eye view (as in the asparagus and bowl-of-salt shots).

instant art

skill level: beginner

MATERIALS

- eight 18-inch canvas stretchers (available at art supply stores)
- 2 pieces of fabric, at least 24 square inches
- staple gun
- scissors
- D-rings
- screwdriver
- picture wire

DIRECTIONS

1. Assemble canvas stretchers into two 18-inch frames. Center assembled stretcher frame over back side of fabric.

2. Pull center of one side of fabric around to back of frame, and staple fabric to back of frame. Pull center of opposite side of fabric taut to frame back and staple in place. Repeat for remaining two sides.

3. Continue pulling fabric to the back of the stretcher and stapling in place about 2 to 3 inches from preceding staples, opposite sides at a time.

4. Clip excess fabric at corners and fold under fabric to miter neatly, and staple in place.

5. Attach D-rings with screwdriver to back of frame and add picture wire, twisting the ends over the wire.

Make instant art in no time. Starting with a remnant of fabric, cut a square 6 inches larger than the size of a frame of stretchers purchased from an art store. Wrap it snugly around the stretchers and staple in place to the back.

egg paintings

skill level: intermediate

MATERIALS

- ruler
- pencil
- 4 ready-made 10x10-inch gallery-wrap canvases (available from online art supply stores)
- painter's tape
- 2-inch paintbrush (for background), plus a variety of small artists' brushes of different sizes
- background paint (we used Sherwin-Williams' Sagey and Kind Green interior latex paint in matte finish)
- acrylic craft paint for eggs (we used Plaid's FolkArt paints in Ivory White, Vintage White, Linen, Nutmeg, Asphaltum)
- palette with small cups to mix paint colors

Do as galleries do—repeat a single image to make a cool quartet. Sketch an egg shape on four ready-made art canvases. Paint the background a neutral sage green or pale blue and fill in the eggs with white paint speckled with brown tones.

DIRECTIONS

1. Using ruler and pencil, measure and mark the center point of each canvas. Draw an elliptical shaped egg around each center point (center point should be about 1 inch from bottom and sides of the egg and 1¼ inches from top).

2. Mask out the egg shapes with painter's tape. Using 2-inch brush, paint front and sides of canvases with Sagey hue. While paint is still wet, apply a top coat to the same area with the Kind Green hue, using alternating brush strokes to create an aged effect and add dimension to background. Allow to dry for three or four hours. Remove painter's tape.

3. To paint eggs, apply a base coat of Ivory White to the first egg shape using a ⅜-inch paintbrush, working very neatly around edges. Let dry for about 15 minutes. Mix Ivory White with Vintage White in palette cups for shade tone. While paint is slightly moist, apply shading to edge of one side of egg, using quick strokes and mottling brush for depth. Let dry for 30 minutes.

4. While paint on egg is drying, mix Linen and Nutmeg colors in another palette cup. Pour only Nutmeg color into another cup. Add small dotted speckles on the egg using the Linen-and-Nutmeg mix with a fine-point paintbrush. Add larger speckles using the Nutmeg color with a slightly larger brush. (For inspiration, Google "speckled egg photos.")

5. To create the second egg, refer back to Step 3 but use Linen as the color base. Let dry for 15 minutes. For shading, mix Linen paint with a drop of Nutmeg color in another palette cup. Apply mottled shading to egg as in Step 3; let dry for 30 minutes. While second egg base color is drying, paint third egg base, using a mix of Linen and Vintage White. For shading, add a small drop of Nutmeg to the paint mix. Paint bases and shading of egg and let dry, as described in Step 3. While paint is drying on third egg, paint the base of fourth egg with Vintage White; add a drop of Asphaltum to the shade mixture for fourth egg and apply as described above. Apply speckles to each egg as described in step 4.

nature arts

There's no master of color, beauty, shape and form greater than Mother Nature. So why not celebrate her plentiful gifts by bringing a few indoors? Round up an armful of azaleas from the garden, flower shop or nursery in spring or gather a smattering of richly colored leaves in fall. Let the flowers' fragile beauty brighten a table for a few days, or press the leaves and frame them, allowing them to enrich a room indefinitely—and without spending a cent. Each new season yields a fresh cache for the taking.

flower planter

skill level: beginner

Growing season may be on hold for a while, but don't let that keep you from cultivating fragrant herbs or bright blooms indoors. Set in a pretty planter like this one, they're sure to lift your spirits even more. Plant one with a hyacinth or amaryllis to add color to a windowsill.

DIRECTIONS **SIZE: 7x7x7 inches**

1. Measure, mark and cut two 7x7-inch pieces, two 7x6-inch pieces and one 6x6-inch piece of plywood.

2. Assemble the wood pieces to form a 7x7-inch square box, overlapping the 6-inch sides of the 7x6-inch pieces with 7x7-inch pieces, gluing the edges and nailing into place along the edge with brads. Insert the bottom piece and glue and nail into place.

3. Cut ten 7-inch-long pieces of ¾-inch-diameter bamboo. Saw about ½ inch into one end of each cut piece of bamboo, splitting the diameter in half. Insert a paring knife into the groove and twist the knife sideways until the bamboo splits. Pull the two halves of the bamboo apart. Repeat with all the other cut pieces. Cut two 8½-inch pieces and two 8¼-inch pieces of ¼-inch-diameter bamboo. Split these pieces in half as well, following the technique described above. Or you may be able to split these pieces with the paring knife alone or with a craft knife. Cut each 8¼-inch piece in half crosswise.

4. Using a miter box and saw, cut the ends of each split ¾-inch-wide piece of bamboo with 45-degree angles that face inward from the top corners. Use the miter box and saw to cut both ends of each 8½-inch piece with 90-degree points. Cut one end of each 4⅛-inch piece with 90-degree points. **(NOTE: These pieces may be thin enough to cut the points with scissors.)**

5. Prime and paint the entire wooden box, inside and out, with two coats of primer and two coats of paint, letting dry between coats. Stain all the bamboo pieces, following manufacturer's instructions.

6. Glue the ¾-inch-wide split bamboo pieces around each edge of each side and along the top, letting one side dry before turning to the next. Glue and place the ¼-inch-wide pieces in an X shape on each side. Using a 1/16-inch drill bit, drill starter holes through each ¾-inch-wide piece of bamboo about 1½ inch from each end. Use brads to attach the pieces securely to the box.

Give your feathered friends a warm welcome with this pretty-as-a-picture birdhouse. With its fresh, clean and easy-to-make design, you'll be as pleased with it as they are.

sweet birdhouse

skill level: intermediate

MATERIALS

- 8-footx8-inchx1-inch clear pine board
- table saw, circular saw, jigsaw or handsaw
- C-clamps (optional)
- miter box and saw (optional)
- wood glue
- hammer and finishing nails
- ⅛-inch-thick Luan
- drill with ¼-inch drill bit and 1³⁄₈-inch hole saw or panel drill bit and flathead screw bit
- router with round router bit (optional)
- palm sander or sandpaper
- wood filler
- putty knife
- paintbrushes
- primer
- paint
- polyurethane (optional)
- 4 black ½-inch flathead screws
- screwdriver (optional)

DIRECTIONS

1. Use a table saw to cut two 12x6½-inch side pieces from the board. If you're using a circular saw, jigsaw or hand saw, clamp the wood to your work surface before cutting. Set the table saw gauge at 45 degrees and cut one short end of each board at a 45-degree angle. Or use a miter box and saw to cut the angles.

2. To make the peaked front and back, cut two 15½x5-inch pieces. Measure and mark the center of one short side on each piece. On front of each piece, measure and mark two lines at 45-degree angles from the center mark toward the side edges. Cut the angles on each board. On front piece, mark position of the hole. Using a drill with the 1⅓-inch hole saw or panel bit, drill a 1³⁄₈-inch hole.

3. Line up the front and back with the side pieces; glue and nail them together, making sure the angle cuts align.

4. To make the roof, cut two 7¼x7-inch pieces and cut both 7¼-inch ends of each piece at 45-degree angles. Glue and nail the two pieces together at the top with the 45-degree angled ends abutting at the peak. Cut two smaller pieces of wood to fit interior of roof and glue them under the roof to fit just inside front and back, enabling roof to stay secure on house, yet allowing it to be removed easily for cleaning.

5. Cut a 5x5-inch bottom piece and glue and nail it in place.

6. Measure, mark and cut a 3x3-inch piece of Luan. Measure, mark and drill four holes ¼ inch from the corners of the Luan piece with a ¼-inch drill bit. Using a drill with the 1⅓-inch hole saw or panel bit, drill a 1³⁄₈-inch hole in the front.

7. Place the Luan piece over the hole on the front and screw into place using a drill driver. Fill all nail holes with wood filler, scraping smooth; let dry. Sand wood filler smooth.

8. Apply two coats of primer to entire roof and house, letting dry between coats. Apply two coats of white paint to front and sides, letting dry between coats. Tape off roof and Luan accent piece, apply two coats blue paint, letting dry. Apply one coat of polyurethane, if desired; let dry.

sunny topiary

skill level: beginner

MATERIALS

- 2 florist oasis foam bricks or, if you're using faux flowers, Styrofoam balls
- serrated knife
- hot-glue gun
- bowl of water (if you're using real flowers)
- medium-size teacup
- straight tree branch, about 15 inches long
- Spanish moss
- large bunch of daisies, real or faux (see Note)
- scissors
- wood skewer

NOTE: Keep real daisies in water while assembling the project.

A sunny topiary with real daisies brightens a mantel, or if you use faux flowers it'll bring cheer all year. Insert a long stick or ribbon-wrapped dowel into the bottom of the daisy-covered ball and stake it in a yellow mug filled with floral foam. Cover the foam with tufts of Spanish moss.

DIRECTIONS

1. If you're using real flowers, cut one foam brick in half crosswise to form two squares. Glue squares together to form cube; let dry.

2. Carve oasis cube into sphere; first trim away corners, then carefully trim edges in curves.

3. Place sphere in bowl of water and soak for 30 minutes.

4. While sphere is soaking, cut second foam brick to fit snugly inside teacup. Remove foam and place small amount of glue on bottom before replacing in cup. Let dry. If you're using faux flowers, cut one Styrofoam ball to fit cup and insert.

5. Push tree branch two-thirds of the way into the foam in the cup. Remove branch and place glue inside hole in foam; replace branch, making sure it is straight. Let dry.

6. Glue moss to cover top of foam in cup.

7. If you're using real flowers, remove sphere from water; press out excess water and reshape. Push ball onto top of branch, about two-thirds of the way. If you're using faux flowers, push the other Styrofoam ball onto the branch.

8. Trim daisy stems about ¾ inch from flower.

9. Using skewer, poke 1-inch-deep hole in top of sphere. Insert one stem into hole.

10. Continue poking holes and inserting daisies into sphere so flowers overlap slightly and foam is completely covered. If you're using faux flowers, you may want to add a dab of glue to the stems before inserting into the ball.

tea towel sachets

skill level: beginner

Chic and functional, these homespun tea towel sachets make great gifts for friends and family. Small squares of vintage fabric are filled with dried balsam, then tied with grosgrain ribbon and topped with a decorative brooch.

MATERIALS

- striped linen fabric or tea towels
- small dinner plate or 10-inch circle template
- pencil
- pinking shears
- 1½-inch-wide grosgrain ribbon
- scissors
- ground balsam (natural moth repellent; available at health-food stores)
- small fresh balsam branches
- vintage rhinestone pins or shoe clips

DIRECTIONS

1. For each sachet, lay linen fabric or tea towels flat and trace plate or template onto fabric; cut out with pinking shears.

2. Cut 6-inch length of grosgrain ribbon.

3. Place several tablespoons of ground balsam in the center of the fabric; gather up and tie with ribbon.

4. Place balsam branch over knot. Attach brooch or shoe clip to cover knot and hold greenery in place.

broom accent

skill level: beginner

Create this decorative and fragrant broom accent with lush sprigs of long-needled pine, secured at the base with a swath of satin ribbon. Tuck in some pepper berries and lemon leaves for a bright splash of color.

MATERIALS

- fresh long-needle pine branches
- rubber band
- pepper berry branches
- lemon leaves
- scissors
- satin ribbon: 1-inch-wide pale green; ¼-inch-wide pale pink
- hot-glue gun

DIRECTIONS

1. Hold pine branches in bundle so branch ends are about 1 inch thick; wrap with rubber band about 3 inches from top so needles form broom.

2. Place pepper berry branches and leaves on top of bundle.

3. Cut 7 inches of green ribbon; drape over the length of bundled ends and glue one end of the ribbon along the front, wrap it over the top and glue the other end over the back to cover top of broom.

4. Glue one end of remaining green ribbon just below rubber band, covering glued ribbon ends from previous step. Wrap this ribbon tightly around the tops of branches over the glued strip of ribbon to form broom handle all the way up and then back down to the rubber band; cut and glue end in place.

5. Wrap pink ribbon around top end of handle; glue end in place.

6. Trim lower ends of needles to form a crisp edge and fan out to form broom shape.

birch candleholders

skill level: intermediate

Bring a calming, natural elegance to your table with these birch candleholders. Cut birch wood into varying lengths and use a router bit on your power drill to carve out holes wide enough to accommodate your favorite pillar candles. Place the candleholders on a mirror to reflect the light, and add an assortment of nuts, rose hips, pepper berries and evergreen sprigs for added color and texture.

MATERIALS

- straight birch logs, about 2 to 4 inches in diameter
- C-clamp
- hand saw
- drill with 1/8-, 1- and 1½-inch-diameter bits
- long upholstery tacks
- assorted candles
- round mirror
- assorted greens, nuts and pepper berry branches

DIRECTIONS

1. Clamp log to work surface; cut to desired height.

2. To make candleholder with lid, cut off a ½-inch slice of one log. Drill several small holes in center of slice; set aside.

3. Using larger bit (1-inch for tall candle; 1½-inch for votive candle), drill hole straight into log, about 1½ inch deep, to hold candle.

4. Attach lid to top of candleholder by pushing a tack through both pieces, close to edge.

5. Place candles in holders. Arrange on mirror, surrounded by greens, nuts and pepper berries.

woodland potpourri

skill level: beginner

MATERIALS

- assorted dried and fresh scented items (we used pinecones, rose hips, cedar shavings, balsam sprigs, cinnamon sticks, allspice berries, whole star anise and bay leaves)
- mixing bowl
- pine essential oil
- decorative glass bowl

DIRECTIONS

1. Place assorted dried and fresh items in mixing bowl.

2. Sprinkle mixture with a few drops of pine essential oil; toss lightly. Add more oil as needed to achieve desired scent.

3. Gently place mixture in decorative bowl.

Keep your home smelling fresh and cozy all season long with a customized blend of your favorite winter scents. For our woodland potpourri, we combined zesty cinnamon sticks and clove with rose hips, cedar shavings, allspice and bay leaves—tossed gently with pine, evergreen essential oils and ground cinnamon for a lasting aroma.

fragrant florals

skill level: beginner

MATERIALS

- vintage ceramic planters in assorted colors
- potting soil
- flower bulbs, such as paperwhites, amaryllis or other flowers recommended for forced winter blooming
- Spanish moss
- small nuts in shells

DIRECTIONS

1. Fill planters halfway with soil; place bulbs in soil, following bulb seller's recommendations for soil type.

2. Place planters in cold dark storage, such as a refrigerator or basement, keeping the soil moist for about 4 weeks before setting out to bloom.

3. Cover soil with moss and nuts.

Vintage ceramic planters are the ideal match for these fragrant florals. Placed in stones and water and exposed to direct sunlight, narcissus and amaryllis bulbs can be coaxed into bloom in just three to four weeks.

plant stand

skill level: beginner

MATERIALS

- hand drill and bits
- wooden stepladder with paint tray, about 5 or 6 feet tall
- sandpaper
- tack cloth
- acrylic paint
- paintbrush
- ruler
- pencil
- 2 small L brackets with hardware
- wall anchors
- hammer

DIRECTIONS

1. Using drill with screwdriver bit, remove back of ladder, leaving paint tray intact.

2. Sand front of ladder. Wipe off dust with tack cloth. Apply two or more coats of paint, letting dry after each coat.

3. Lean ladder against wall; mark bracket placement on wall and on underside of both sides of top step of ladder. Remove ladder. Drill pilot holes in wall, hammer in wall anchors and screw in place to attach brackets to wall.

4. Drill pilot holes in ladder. Lean ladder against wall in alignment with brackets and screw in place to attach brackets to ladder.

Deconstructed and brightly painted, an old ladder gets new life as a charming plant stand.

PHOTO CREDITS

Lucas Allen: 56.

Courtesy of Art.com: 92.

Andre Baranowski: 120.

Gordon Beall: 62.

Colleen Duffley: 54.

John Gruen: 8, 11, 12, 16, 18, 24, 84, 90, 91, 104, 106, 107, 109, 110, 112, 113.

Aimee Herring: 14, 20, 22, 36, 40, 41, 69, 70, 72, 73, 74, 76, 78, 86, 87, 88, 93, 96, 98, 108, 105, 116, 118.

Jeff McNamara: 38, 46, 68, 111.

Steven Mays: 58.

Keith Scott Morton: 48, 89.

Jennifer Newbery Mead: 122, 123, 124, 125, 126.

Deborah Ory: 26, 34, 35, 44, 77, 127.

Michael Partenio: 19, 80.

Eric Roth: 63.

Joe Schmelzer: 85, 94, 100, 102.

Kate Sears: 10, 23, 27, 30, 60, 64, 65.

Michael Weschler: 50.

Paul Whicheloe: 32, 42.

RESOURCES

Behr
Behr.com

Covington
Covington-newyork.com

Fairfield Processing
www.poly-fil.com

Plaid Enterprises
Plaidonline.com

Pratt & Lambert
prattandlambert.com

Shutterfly
Shutterfly.com

Skil Tools
Skiltools.com

Therm O Web
Thermoweb.com

Thibaut
Thibautdesign.com

Yaley Enterprises
Yaley.com

ACKNOWLEDGMENTS

The talent and energy of several people went into the making of this book and all deserve our acknowledgement and thanks. Much of the reporting on or development of these projects was done by regular contributors to the *Woman's Day* Special Interest Publications, Pamela Acuff and Michele Filon as well as staff associate editor Ayn-Monique Tetreault-Rooney Klahre. A number of crafters and stylists have also contributed to the projects in these pages, including Ingrid Leess, Amy Leonard, Matthew Levinson, Dan Pasky, Ginevra Pylant and Donna Talley. Special thanks also go to Dorothée Walliser and Karen Rosenthall for shepherding this book through its development and publication.